Parallax Press
P.O. Box 7355
Berkeley, California 94707
www.parallax.org

Parallax Press is the publishing division
of Unified Buddhist Church, Inc.

Edited by Rachel Neumann
Illustrations by Jason DeAntonis
Cover and text design by Jess Morphew
Author Photo by Natascha Bruckner

Library of Congress Cataloging-in-Publication Data

Murray, Zachiah.
  Mindfulness in the garden : Zen tools for digging in the dirt / Zachiah
Murray.
     p. cm.
  Includes bibliographical references.
  ISBN 978-1-937006-15-0
  1. Gardening. 2. Gardening--Philosophy. 3. Zen Buddhism. I. Title.
SB454.3.P45M87 2012
  635--dc23
                      2012013163

1 2 3 4 5 / 16 15 14 13 12

MINDFULNESS IN THE GARDEN

GARDEN

ZEN TOOLS FOR DIGGING IN THE DIRT

ZACHIAH MURRAY

Foreword by Thich Nhat Hanh

Illustrated by Jason DeAntonis

PARALLAX PRESS

To Nature

CONTENTS

FOREWORD

Thich Nhat Hanh

The garden is a perfect place to practice mindfulness. Watering, planting, touching the earth, and letting your fingers feel the soil are wonderfully restorative activities. Even if you live in a crowded city, find a place where you can hoe the earth, plant herbs or vegetables and take care of flowers. You can cultivate a patch of grass, a small plot, or just a wooden box. I like to spend time gardening every day. I enjoy growing lettuce, tomatoes, and other vegetables. Gardening reminds us that the things we throw away can become compost that will turn into beautiful flowers and nourishing herbs, fruits, and vegetables.

Mindfulness practice is based on our deep awareness of the present moment. So many of us feel alienated because we've lost our awareness of the interconnectedness of all things. In the garden, we are surrounded by beautiful examples of our relationship with nature. We can see how the sun, the rain, the compost, and the earth all need to come together to create the rose. When we look deeply at fresh vegetables, we can see not only the sun in them, but thousands of other phenomena as well. If there were no clouds, there would be no rainwater. Without water, air, and soil, there would be no vegetables.

Garbage can smell terrible, especially when it's rotting organic matter. But it can also become rich compost for fertilizing the garden. With mindfulness, we see that the fragrant rose and the stinking garbage are two sides of the same existence. Without one, the other cannot be. Everything is in transformation. The rose that wilts after six days will become part of the garbage. And after six months, the garbage will be transformed into a rose.

In each one of us there is compassion and love, and there is anger, fear, discrimination, and jealousy. When we see the difficult elements in us, we tend to think of them as garbage. We want to pretend they don't exist and just focus on the beautiful things. But we don't need to panic. As good gardeners, we know that with awareness, care, and compassion we can transform these difficulties into nourishing compost and, eventually, flowers and beauty will reappear.

Gardening teaches us that whatever we water will grow. When we offer water to a plant, we offer it to the whole Earth. When watering plants, if we speak to them, we are also speaking to ourselves and to the world. The plant takes refuge in the earth. Whether the plant grows well or not, depends on how much nourishment it can get from the sun, soil, and water. Our mindful attention is like the water. Our emotions and perceptions are seeds within us. If we water the anger and fear within us, they will grow like the weeds. Alternatively, we can water the flowers of compassion, understanding, and love.

The garden reminds us that how we are in our lives is up to us. When we garden with mindfulness, every time we breathe in, we will know we are breathing in. Every time we breathe out, we will know we are breathing out. In this way, we are fully ourselves. We are the master gardeners in our own beautiful garden.

INTRODUCTION

Tucked in the far left corner of my childhood home lived a handsome row of silvery-green-leafed Russian olive trees, *Elaeagnus angustifolia*. Beneath their thorny boughs—young knees to the ground and body in an earthly bow—I became a gardener at the tender age of eight. Gardening without gloves, I loved the feel of the earth in my hands: its rich, aromatic texture, warmed by the sun. I still do.

I surrendered many childhood struggles at the feet of those olive trees. I found solace in their silent presence. Grateful for their company, I instinctively knew my survival was intimately connected to theirs. As I stepped away from the carefully tended band of soil that held the olive tree roots firm to the earth, I saw the rich brown soil free from the tangle of weeds that once claimed its clarity. In this clearing, the knot in my mind loosened, and my heart was put at ease.

Now, many years into my practice as a landscape architect, gardening remains a true love. Nature is a place where I come back to myself. Whether it's a window box, vegetable crop, fruit orchard, vineyard, a designed "outdoor room," or simply a patch of tenacious weeds, a garden is the critical demarcation between what is wild and what is cultivated. When we garden—weeding, pre-

paring the soil, planting, watering, tending, harvesting—
we place ourselves at the edge, between what is wild
and what is cultivated. Crossing the garden's threshold,
we enter into a direct relationship with nature and with
ourselves. This is a relationship that must be recognized
and consciously and compassionately entered. It requires
that we garden with a heartfelt mindfulness.

This book offers simple short verses, called
gathas, to guide our gardening and assist us
in becoming present. Zen Master Thich
Nhat Hanh says that reciting a gatha
"helps us to dwell in the present moment
and to be deeply aware of the action we are
doing so that we can perform it with understanding and love." Each gatha waters the seeds of mindfulness within us, softening and cultivating the ground of
our ability to be present.

Each gatha offered is designed to be practiced in
alignment with the breath. First, read the whole gatha,
then, consider inhaling as you recite one line to your-
self and exhale as you recite the next. So the first line
would be in sync with your inhale, the second with your
exhale, the third with your inhale, and the fourth with
your exhale.

Practicing in this way, each four line gatha becomes a gateway to a moment of mindfulness. What is mindfulness? Mindfulness is the awareness of what is around us and within us in the present moment. Looking deeply, and being with what is, frees us from getting caught in the past or the future. When we garden, the details of nature call to life all of our senses grounding us in the present moment. While weeding, for example, we use our sight to discern the beautiful glistening leaves of the native, noninvasive Redwood sorrel (*Oxalis oregana*) from the flat, green, stippled leaves of the invasive sour grass (*Oxalis pes-caprae* L.). We use our sense of taste as we nibble on a basil leaf or bite into a freshly picked, sun-warmed peach. We feel nature's touch as we are gently brushed by the summer's refreshing breeze upon our skin, cooling the perspiration of our labors of love in the garden. Attuned to our breath, we can smell the arrival of the seasons upon the wind. As we see, hear, smell, taste, and feel nature's details, we become more present, and compassion and love grow within us. Gardening mindfully—being present with our shovels, our steps, and our gathas—we invite the mind to drop into the heart, and the tangle of our thoughts is loosened.

chapter 1

ENTERING THE GARDEN

Entering the garden
I see my true nature.
In its reflection
my heart is at peace.

We cross many thresholds in our lives. Some thresholds are monumental—being born, learning to walk, starting school, graduating, getting our first job, losing our first job, getting married, giving birth, and dying. Other thresholds are subtle—moving from one room to another, passing through a gate, or crossing an intersection.

When we enter a garden, we are crossing a threshold into nature. William Longgood wrote, "A garden is a portal, a passage into another world of your own thoughts and your own making."[4] Our entryway into the garden may be unusual, such as an old architecturally rendered door salvaged from a garage sale, an ornately detailed wrought iron gate, or a lovely wooden arbor adorned with our favorite wisteria vine draping with its magnificent fragrant purple flowers. It may be an understated entryway, such as a simple change in pavement, a single row of fresh boxwood shrubs opening in their middle like a low wall, or the boughs of two maple trees creating an arch in nature's blue-sky ceiling while dappling their shade upon the earth.

Bold or subtle, a threshold into the garden gives us just enough space to come back to ourselves. It is a place where we shed our time-focused, goal-driven pace. We slow down, and we enter the present moment. Crossing this threshold mindfully, we make the transition from the mundane into the sanctuary of our garden. As

4 Peg Streep, *Spiritual Gardening: Creating Sacred Space Outdoors* (Makawao, Maui: Inner Ocean Publishing, Inc., 1999), 9.

we enter our garden, we arrive. We can stop here and follow our in-breath and our out-breath, observe the beauty and grace of the plants around us, and become deeply present.

Entering the garden,
Breathing in, we bring our full awareness to the moment of our arrival.

I see my true nature.
As we breathe out, we realize our direct communion with all of nature, and we understand ourselves more deeply.

In its reflection
Breathing in, we see that the beauty and magnificence of our garden is a mirror of our own beauty and magnificence.

my heart is at peace.
Alive in the present moment, held in the arms of nature, and knowing our direct communion with life, we breathe out and our hearts are at peace.

LOOKING AT A TREE

Looking deeply at the tree,
I feel its presence.
In its stillness,
I find my true being.

The wind-blown architecture of a cypress tree growing at the ocean's edge does not judge how our hair looks in the morning. Instead, it can remind us of the elegant beauty that appears when we allow nature to sculpt us. The clouds in the sky do not begrudge us our moods, but instead they model for us a way to simply be with what is and express it completely, as they move from bright billowy white to the soggy drab grey foretelling of rain's arrival. Our tears become the rain falling from their tender underbellies. The wily pumpkin stealthily growing on top of our fence does not complain that it is not on the ground with its brothers and sisters, but grows courageously where it finds itself. Nature just is, and it teaches us how to simply be.

Like the elements of our garden, it is our nature to be that which we already are. Landscape Architect Lawrence Halprin wrote, "Since we are a part of nature… we empathize deeply with its ways…they serve as unconscious models of how things should be."[5] The

---

5   Kathleen Norris Brenzel, *Sunset Western Garden Book*
      (Menlo Park, CA: Sunset Publishing Corporation, 2001), 18.

buzz of a bee, the rustling of an aspen's leaves as they blow in the wind, the nighttime rhythm of cicadas—this is nature's voice, unencumbered by any need to change or improve.

Nature is the master of being. It knows nothing other than to simply be itself—vast, infinite, and unconditional. If we want to learn how to be, we need to spend time with the Master: nature itself. Looking deeply at a tree—branches reaching toward the sky, trunk straight and strong, roots winding deeply into the ground—we feel its presence, and we honor its place in our garden. The tree carries the ancient wind, the sea's rain, and the sun of many years within itself. Its profound presence arrives in us as stillness. Breathing mindfully, we embody this stillness. Becoming still like the tree, our thoughts can be left at the garden's gate and we can simply be ourselves.

Looking deeply at the tree,
Breathing in, we witness the tree in all its beauty.

I feel its presence.
Branches reaching toward the sky, trunk straight and strong, roots winding deep into the ground—we feel the tree's presence. Breathing out, we honor its place in our garden.

In its stillness,
The tree carries the wind, the rain, and the sun of many years. Its profound presence arrives in us as stillness. Breathing in, we embody this stillness.

I find my true being.
Breathing out, we arrive in our true state of being. Nowhere to go, nothing to do; we just are.

WALKING IN THE GARDEN

Sole to soil, I touch the earth.
In this communion,
my soul finds
a true friend.

Set your intention to walk mindfully. Take a few deep breaths and just acknowledge that during your walk you will try to be aware of your environment and your internal state, your thoughts, feelings, and sensations. As you begin to walk, first notice the sensation of each foot as it touches the ground. Witness the process of moving your legs. What muscles tense or relax as you move? Observe where you are stepping and the quality of each step. Expand your awareness to include your surroundings. As you walk, what do you see, smell, hear, taste, and feel? How does the air feel on your skin? Expand your awareness so that you remain aware of the sensation of walking and the external environment around you, while you also become aware of your internal experiences, such as your thoughts and emotions. What thoughts cross your mind as you walk? There's no need to judge these internal experiences. Just notice them for what they are.

With our mindful walking we enter into a direct communion with the earth and with the ancient practices and rituals of the cultures buried beneath our highways and skyscrapers. We slow down. We excavate ourselves from the insulation and isolation of our daily routines as we bring our sole to the soil, mindfully connecting our steps and our movements with our in-breath and our out-breath.

We can make every step we walk in the garden a mindful step, one taken slowly and in connection with our breath. This is true wherever we walk in the world, but particularly so in the garden, where we are walking directly on the soil instead of on human-imposed materials such as concrete or asphalt. Touching the earth directly, we become more aware not only of the life above the ground, but also of the immense expression of life below the earth's surface.

Consider the earthworm. It has five hearts called aortic arches, and it plays a vital role, providing passageways for water, oxygen, and nutrients to reach our plants' root systems by creating space within the soil. Five hearts! Every time I come across an earthworm while I am gardening, I say, "Hello there, thank you for the wonderful work you are doing." I handle it with tenderness and love, tucking it back into the soil for protection from the sun's glare, and perhaps from becoming a meal for an opportunistic robin rambling nearby. As a young child walking to school on a rainy day, long before I knew how instrumental earthworms were to the survival of the earth's flora, I would pick up all the struggling worms I found on the sidewalk and street as I walked. Despite their slippery, squiggling bodies I carefully placed them in neighboring flowerbeds, preventing them from being crushed by our shoes and our tires.

Many of us long to return to our childlike curiosity and openness. Zen Master Thich Nhat Hanh says, "Getting in touch with true mind is like digging deep in the soil and reaching a hidden source that fills our well with fresh water."[6] What we seek in this excavation, albeit perhaps unconsciously, is ourselves. With the advancement of technology and construction all around us, we have gained instant access across the globe via the internet and our many ways of traveling; however, most of us have lost contact with ourselves. Many of us lie buried beneath the tundra of our technological advances and our busyness. The slow, intentional cadence of mindful walking frees us from the tangle of serpentine electrical cords coiled beneath our desk. It returns us to the heart of life and restores our childlike

6   Thich Nhat Hanh, *Interbeing: Fourteen Guidelines for Engaged Buddhism* (Berkeley, CA: Parallax Press, 1998), 3.

wonder. We begin to see the jewel-like dew on the garden spider's web with fresh eyes. We hear the mockingbird's melodious song with fresh ears, and we smell the orange tree's blossoms with our fresh in-breath. We learn to live in the present moment, and we come alive.

Sole to soil, I touch the earth.
Breathing in, we slow down.

In this communion,
Breathing out, we are free from the busyness of our lives and the serpentine cords living beneath our desks. We enjoy our freedom communing in nature.

my soul finds
Breathing in, we relax into nature's welcoming embrace, and we come to know our garden and ourselves.

a true friend.
Breathing out, we build a true friendship with the Earth and all its inhabitants.

chapter 2

SEEING GREEN

Inside the garden's gate
a sea of green surrounds me.
In its embrace I see
the truth of oneness.

Our garden conspires to wake us up. The land is already whole and complete. It wants nothing more from us than our pure attention. Spending time in nature's fold, we allow the sea of green to hold us, and we relax into its many layers and textures. Our movements slow down, and we begin to walk, to breathe, and to garden with mindfulness. Looking with the eyes of mindfulness, our entire existence is reflected back to us in the repetition of nature's seasons, its patterns, and the undeniable exchange of oxygen and carbon dioxide that sustains the life within us. Walking, breathing, and gardening without trying to control things, we are carried by the Earth. She meets us at every step.

Our own continuation is witnessed in the circle of nature's seasons. The flowers of spring and the pure potential of the seed are reflections of our physically coming into form, embodying life and movement. Our childhood is the garden's summer vegetables, full of delight, growth, and maturing. The fruits and rewards of adulthood are harvested in our gardens' fall season with the maturing of corn, tomatoes, and potatoes. In winter, life swings full circle, as the aging leaves hover and spin to the ground, symbolizing our body's own sacred journey of returning to the earth.

Mindful gardening slowly removes the seemingly solid boundaries surrounding nature's elements and ourselves. We begin to see how we are woven into the earth's fabric through our bodies and our very breath. With our awareness in the present moment, we merge with nature. In its embrace, we know we are never alone.

Inside the garden's gate
Our garden is a sanctuary where we can learn to embody the Earth's ancient wisdom. Breathing in, we allow ourselves to enter nature's gate, and we open ourselves to knowing its truth.

a sea of green surrounds me.
Breathing out, we give ourselves to the sea of green that is our garden.

In its embrace I learn to see
Breathing in, we know we are woven into the earth's fabric through our bodies and our breath. We are the flower and the flower is us.

the truth of oneness.
Breathing out, we deeply acknowledge our oneness with life itself.

LEARNING THE
LANGUAGE OF THE LAND

Nature speaks in symbols:
sights, sounds, scents, tastes, and feelings.
Immersed in the language of the land
I embody nature's wisdom.

Nature speaks in the vibrant, arched colors of the rainbow, in the rustling bellies of leaves upon the wind, and in the full-throated, trumpet call of a male peacock, steam rising from his wide open mouth. It speaks to us in the fresh scent of green earth, in moistening raindrops tapping tunes upon the Earth's skin, the humming of a bumblebee as it floats from poppy to poppy, joyfully circling its body around the golden stamens pregnant with pollen, and in the voice of an apple's red skin. Its language is the blooming of rosebuds into the petals of brilliant feather-like beings, the unfurling of lush star-shaped leaves as the sweetgum tree's native summer garb, and the decadence of a shiny blue bowl full of rich golden and brown stippled pears.

To hear nature's voice we need to be settled and quiet inside ourselves. Practicing mindful gardening drops our center to the Earth's hearth. Grounded in nature, our mind becomes quiet and we become still. We take the time to look, to listen, to smell, to feel, and to sense all that is around us. Words and labels lose their grip on us. Completely given to the act of deep listening— free of naming things—we become immersed in the voice of nature. The natural integrity of the land and its inhabitants, expressing themselves without pause and without judgment, loosens our own throats.

Sun and shadow, wind and stillness, water and drought, green and brown, up and down, cold and hot, soft and hard, smooth and rough, are the expressions and the native tongue of the land. Gently holding our intentions for our garden close to the cheek of the Earth, we keep an open and mindful eye, ear, and heart for nature's voice to guide us. Listening deeply, immersed in the language of the land, we breathe in nature's wisdom.

Nature speaks in symbols:
Breathing in, we hear nature's voice in the movement of the wind, the rushing of a river, and the glow of the moon.

sights, sounds, scents, tastes, and feelings.
Breathing out, we allow ourselves to be absorbed by the details and symbols of nature and the land.

Immersed in the language of the land,
Listening deeply, immersed in the language of the land, we breathe in nature's wisdom. Free of our thoughts and preconceived ideas, present only to the moment, we take it all into ourselves, and allow it to inform our movements as we garden.

I embody nature's wisdom.
With nature's wisdom as the source of our inspiration and actions, we become authentic gardeners. Breathing out, our thoughts, words, and actions are nature's continuation in our garden's growth.

DESIGN AND INSPIRATION

Sights and sounds, scents and textures,
and the stillness of silence—
beauty, beauty everywhere—
I treasure each drop.

All around us, the natural world offers its beauty for
our reflection and integration into our lives and our
gardens. As a landscape architect, I get inspiration for
my designs by going into nature and observing the
lines, movements, colors, and forms I find in the outdoor world. Without regular time in nature, my design
runs the risk of becoming stagnant and unresponsive.
Whether we are designing our first or our hundredth
garden, we can be inspired by the naturally occurring
lines, forms, rocks, flowers, trees, and waters all around
us. Witnessing the lovely combination of purple salvia
with bright yellow *Stella d'oro* daylilies in a neighbor's
garden may inspire us to use purple and yellow in the
color palette for our own garden. The delicate presence
of flowering dogwood along the edge of a redwood for-
est may guide us to the perfect place for a dogwood in
our backyard. Nature is our constant companion and
muse as we contemplate the design and layout of our
own garden.

Each of us has an inner garden designer. Our
inner designer can be inspired by a stroll in the park

or through an unfamiliar neighborhood, observing the gardens. The cultivated landscape of an arboretum and the abundant stock of a nursery are amazing resources for learning about new plants we may have never seen. As we stroll and discover, we fill the creative well of our inner designer, and our garden begins to take form in our imagination.

Whether we are new to gardening or have been digging in the dirt for years, filling the well is a rich time of gathering new knowledge and ideas. There is no substitute for spending time in and with nature as a source of freshness for the underground stream of inspiration running deep within us. Visually experiencing gardens and images opens doors within us and makes available ideas we may have never considered possible. Taking notes and drawing pictures brings these experiences to a deeper level within our bodies, and informs the direction of our gardening in a very real way.

Replenishing our creativity is an active process, one in which we remain awake and aware. Learning what attracts and repels us is a valuable part of filling our creative reservoir; this discernment helps us to understand our relationship with the natural world. Whether we are experiencing nature while on a walk or through pictures in magazines, it's important that we take notice of what we like and what we don't like. Writing out our responses—noting why we are drawn or repelled by certain elements we observe—is vital to our gathering, and keeps us engaged in our exploration. Our notes

reveal patterns within ourselves that have an impact on our relationship to the natural world. These patterns may reflect not only our likes and dislikes, but also may reveal what brings us comfort or discomfort, joy or sorrow, energy or lethargy. Remaining awake and aware, we observe our preferences without judgment.

While observing form is integral to our creative process, our inner garden designer is also deeply nourished by silence. The gift of silence allows us to hear the still small voice of the heart—our authentic self—and places us in direct attunement with nature's stillness. The stillness of nature's being finds residence inside of us. Recognizing our self as the stillness invites spaciousness and grace to flow into our vision. Because there is infinitely more silence than there is sound, silence is a vast playground for our imagination to nourish itself. Whole new worlds, and gardens, spring from the pure potential of silence.

Sights and sounds, scents and textures,
Breathing in, we fill our creative reservoir with the sight of a dragonfly, the sound of the red-legged frog's chirp, the scent of lavender, and the texture of freshly shucked

corn on the palm of our hand. Each detail informs our vision for our garden.

and the stillness of silence—
Breathing out, we allow ourselves to become silent, listening for our heart's inspiration for our vision.

beauty, beauty everywhere—
Breathing in, we mindfully take in the beauty of the natural world filling our creative well with the living inspiration of the landscape surrounding us.

I treasure each drop.
Breathing out, we are awake and aware in the active process of co-creating our garden with nature.

DISCERNING THE SACRED

Seeing things as they are,
I listen closely to my devotional heart.
Following my inner joy,
I discern what is sacred.

The first step in discerning what is sacred to us—that which we will preserve—in our existing garden is to allow our heart full reign. The heart has both a devotional nature and a wisdom, or discerning, nature. Facts and reasoning can drown out the guidance of our emotional knowing. If we go straight to facts and reasoning about what plants are easiest, or what does best with the sun and water and natural resources of the space, we may never hear our heart's voice. It's important to know what we care about first without having to be reasonable.

This may not sound wise; however, we need to know how we feel. We need to know that the cherry tree our grandfather gave us is important *even if* it is scrawny and tattered looking. A greater intimacy with nature is born of our willingness to look deeply. As we allow our devotion to take residence in our garden we are more an integral part of the whole of it. Knowing our sentimental attachments gives us greater insight about the direction of our garden's form once dovetailed with the necessary and more linear, factual analysis of our garden.

We give our devotion a space in our garden when we allow ourselves to acknowledge our emotions, our sentimental attachments, and our joy. This is our truth. It is not wise to ignore any part of our truth. Placing judgment aside, we allow ourselves to know the full depth of our emotional sentimental selves regarding our land. Later in the process, we will balance this devotional knowing with the facts—our more linear, factual observations—but first we need to know where we stand. Knowing our truth keeps us honest and authentic in our decisions as we begin to give our garden form.

Seeing things as they are,
With this breath we simply allow ourselves to be with
what is—the good, the bad, the beautiful, and the ugly.
We allow equanimity to be the ground from which we
observe.

I listen closely to my devotional heart.
Breathing out, we allow ourselves to listen deeply to our
heart's devotional response to the land.

Following my inner joy,
 Our joy is the harbinger of what is sacred to us. We
listen for our inner joy to inform our movements, our
decisions, and our discernment of what is valuable. We
let go of reason, and allow ourselves to simply know
what brings us delight, comfort, and satisfaction without having to justify it to anyone—not even ourselves.

I discern what is sacred.
That which delights us is sacred regardless of its form.
Breathing out, we water the seed of self-acceptance and
love within ourselves.

chapter 3

DESIGNING YOUR GARDEN

*In this vision,
I see clearly
the entire universe
humbly unfold.*

Allowing form and non-form to unite happens as we bring our vision down to earth to meet our existing land and its inhabitants. For me as an architect, one of the most exciting parts of the creative process is holding the hand of existing forms while simultaneously holding the hand of creative vision yet to be manifest. By holding the hand of form, we embrace the land and all its natives—trees, shrubs, flowers, birds, ladybugs, and lizards—as they are, keeping in mind our experience and feelings about them. In the midst of holding the hand of the existing forms of our garden, we also hold the hand of our creative self. This is our inner garden designer that has observed nature, taken in its details, its patterns, and its way of being; it is the hand of our imagination.

Infinite potential lives between the existing forms of our garden and our creative vision for it. We, as gardeners, stand on holy ground uniting the hand of existing form with the non-form hand of our imagination. We begin to give our ideas and vision physical expression when we draw them. Whether we etch our ideas into our garden's brown soil, using the heel of our boot, sketch them onto a napkin during a dinner gathering with friends, or place pencil to paper carefully drafting the images that inspire us, we are now beginning to shape our garden. Once visible, the lines of our vision breathe their first breath into life. Upon the land the scribbled or meticulous lines of our vision jump into three-dimensional bed edges and raised planter boxes. Circles drawn on a napkin pop up into lilacs and lavender planted in the earth. Putting our ideas into drawings allows us to see and mindfully consider spatial relationships between and among the elements of our proposed vision and our existing landscape. Symbolically, our drawings capture a snapshot of our initial vision like a frame in the film of an old-time movie reel. Given time, the movie reel will unwind itself telling the rest of the story, and the seeds of our vision will mature into their fullest expression as our garden unfolds.

Careful to be mindful during our creative process, we study the parts of our garden while also considering the whole. Putting our ideas into drawings allows us to see and mindfully consider spatial relationships between and among the elements of our proposed vision and our existing landscape. An important rule to always keep in mind is *form follows function*. It is important not to force our ideas on the land, but to be supple and flexible in our approach. When we allow the forms of our vision to follow their function we have the greatest chance of working in harmony with the naturally occurring conditions allowing our design be successful. For example, if we had envisioned a simple level walkway from the street to our front porch, but find there is a steady slope that exists across the yard—form following function—we will need to incorporate a set of steps or an accessible ramp to accommodate the change in elevation. Realizing our vision will need to conform to our land, we take time to study how our new lines relate to the existing terrain and inhabitants of our garden, and we allow a design to evolve with the natural contours and conditions of the land. We walk around inside our imagined forms, feeling deeply into their structure, their size, and their relationship to the earth. Our drawings provide a place where we can return to reassess, to check in, and to make changes when necessary.

Transcribing our vision into drawn form sets the foundation for our garden to grow, allowing us to trust the creative process. Planted in the soil of trust, our vision can take form naturally and organically. Mindfully drawing the lines and forms of our vision frees us.

In this vision
Breathing in, our vision gives fresh life to our garden.

I see clearly
Our drawings help us see clearly how all the elements of our garden and nature itself can work together in harmony.

the entire universe
Breathing in, we acknowledge the presence of the universe in our humble garden.

humbly unfold.
Breathing out, our garden unfolds according to nature's laws and the lay of our land.

VISION MEETS VENERABLES

Holding my vision loosely,
I lay it with love upon the earth.
The seed of my creativity is watered,
as my imagination meets life.

Having discovered what is sacred to us through our joy, we turn to discerning what is strong and functioning through the dispassionate wisdom of our hearts. The natural thriving of existing life guides our process of discernment. The presence of health in our natives indicates their relative harmony with the environment, whereas disease points to a level of dis-ease in the existing conditions. As we look closely at the flora and fauna of our land, we understand more intimately the organic condition in which our garden lives and thrives. With the eyes of our wise and discerning hearts we come to terms with what is working and what is not. We take note as we lovingly place our vision loosely upon the land. We see where our vision and our venerables are in harmony, and where their juxtaposition creates struggle or conflict.

Perhaps we identify a place where our cherished apricot irises, given to us by our great-grandmother, will perish under the canopy of heavy shade created by a proposed redwood (*Sequoia sempervirens*) once it matures. Seeing the potential disharmony, we can compromise by choosing a different tree that offers less shade, such as the filtered shade of the deciduous Sweetbay Magnolia (*Magnolia virginiana*). During the summer the magnolia's graceful, dappled shade will allow sunlight to reach our prized irises, and during the winter it will give the irises full sun to encourage their bloom come spring. We may decide, however, to allow our venerable irises to reign supreme by abandoning the idea of having a tree near them at all, allowing them to continue prospering a plethora of apricot blooms by heeding their natural inclination for full sun. When there is a conflict between our vision for our garden, including its location, size, or form, and the existing plants and animals already inhabiting the land, we have an opportunity to bring our mindfulness practice and our vision together in finding a creative solution that both protects what is sacred to us while simultaneously preserving the integrity of our design. Together joy and discernment allow our garden, and our hearts, to thrive.

Holding my vision loosely,
Breathing in, we expand our lungs and we relax. Mind and body soften with our breath; we loosen our grip on our well-thought-out plans; and we allow our joy and discernment to be equal partners in the unfolding of our garden.

I lay it with love upon the earth.
Breathing out, our vision meets the rich earth.

The seed of my creativity is watered,
Breathing in, form and function intertwine.

as my imagination meets life.
Breathing out, the visible and invisible weave a tapestry that before did not exist, and new life takes root where we stand.

THE GRACEFUL LINE OF CLARITY

With my heart's discernment,
clarity sows itself into my garden's soil.
In the stream of grace,
a new world blooms into being.

A line of clarity reveals itself to us as we place our heart's discernment upon the hearth and truth of the Earth's soil. With time and equanimity, this line of insight reveals itself to us naturally. We need not force it. As we listen to, observe, and respond authentically to our garden and our vision, we enter the stream of grace. Immersed in grace, our hearts remain calm and peaceful as a new world blooms into being. Grounded in our practice of nonattached witnessing and midwifery, we allow that which had never before existed to grow. One step at a time, our garden is given life. Given the grace of nature's unfoldment, our garden blossoms into manifestation, taking a form that holds both our heart and our intellect. We are our garden's midwife, as it blooms into its fullest expression, an expression that is often much more than we could ever have imagined.

With my heart's discernment,
Breathing in, our steps and movements are filled with the peace of knowing that our garden is the result of careful listening, deep discernment, and wise visioning.

clarity sows itself into my garden's soil.
The natural character of the land and our vision weave a tapestry of beauty into the sanctuary of our garden. Breathing out, responding authentically, we allow nature's clarity to take root.

In the stream of grace,
Breathing in, we acknowledge the expansive creative potential of working with life on life's terms. This is joining in the flow of grace.

a new world blooms into being.
Breathing out, we know our breath is the breath of life itself, and the pure potential of our vision blooms into being.

chapter 4

RISKING
THE TANGLE

Form and non-form have spun their threads.
Together they inform my movements.
The web of their wisdom holds me,
as I risk the tangle that is my garden and myself.

One of the most dynamic moments of creating our garden sanctuary is the point at which we step onto the land, ready to face the physical reality of bringing our vision to life. The sun touches down on our backs and assures us it will be our companion as we make our humble movements on the Earth's skin.

We often begin in a tangle of weeds that we have neglected to govern and control for several seasons, if not longer. Weeding is a mindfulness meditation, one that takes patience and love. It is our chosen task now to give guidance to and set boundaries for our weeds. Risking the tangle of our garden, we enter the terrain of our inner landscape as well. There, reflected in the tangle of our garden, lie the knotted up thoughts and feelings of our minds—stories we tell ourselves over and over causing ourselves, and others, to suffer.

If we are mindful about how we address the weeds of our garden, we may catch a glimpse of how we deal with our innermost emotional landscape. Are we frustrated and angry as we pull our weeds? Does our internal dialog become self-critical or defacing? Are the weeds we are pulling, and the thoughts we harbor, our enemies, or are they signposts for us to turn toward our garden and ourselves with compassion? We can allow our external garden to lead us to profound insights about the inner terrain of our emotional selves, and as our garden becomes clear, so too, do our minds have an opportunity to reclaim their innate clarity.

Gaining clarity means facing the tangle—that is at

once our garden and ourselves—with kindness. If we are harsh with the bristly thorns of thistle, they will assuredly be biting and rash in return. Lashing back with full sting, their laser sharp points can penetrate easily through our gloves. However, as we learn to work with the thorns in our garden—inner and outer—we learn to embrace them without harming ourselves. Giving our full attention to the thistle's thorns we can observe they have a direction and a natural way of growing on the plant's limbs. Holding them firmly but gently at their base, we can skillfully and tenderly remove them from our garden.

Seeing the thistle as not separate from ourselves, it symbolizes those aspects of our inner terrain that need our tending, too. By turning towards our difficult emotions and feelings as we do with our weeds, we gain insight and understanding into them—their source, their direction, and their underlying needs. In learning how to handle the thorns of our garden, we learn how to mindfully embrace our more difficult emotions such as anger, greed, and jealousy, removing their long-held roots inside of us.

Form and non-form have spun their threads.
Breathing in, our vision meets the physical reality of our existing landscape.

Together they inform my movements.
Breathing out, we trust we have authentically entered

the creative process as we allow our insights to guide our decisions and the direction of our garden's unfolding.

The web of their wisdom holds me,
Breathing in, the web of life holds us as we make space in our garden for new life by removing the tangle of weeds that no longer serve us.

as I risk the tangle that is my garden and myself.
Breathing out, we make space in our garden and in ourselves.

BEGINNING TO WEED

Aware of the weeds in my garden,
I start where I am.
In their clearing,
the tangle of my mind is loosened.

Often our initial endeavors in our garden place us face to face with weeds that have tenaciously taken up vast amounts of real estate, leaving hardly a breath of space for the beauties of our vision to grow. Overcoming both the external weeds and the internal chaos can initially feel daunting. It requires us to start where we are with the openness and courage of a beginner's mind. In the grace of our garden is an ever-unfolding mirror of our inner landscape, and in the clearing of the weeds—knees to earth and fingers to thorns—we find space to breathe and grow.

Authentically entered, the garden is a place we go to not to admire our skillfulness as gardeners but to learn how to be mindful and to transform our suffering into beautiful flowers. As we clear our gardens with our shovels, our trowels, and our hoes, we clear ourselves. From each flower, tree, rock, and weed, we learn the openness of the beginner's mind.

Aware of the weeds in my garden,
Breathing in, we meet our weeds without judgment.

I start where I am.
Breathing out, we are fresh.

In their clearing,
Breathing in, we are nourished by the refreshing openness of our garden's soil and the spaciousness created in our weeds' absence.

the tangle of my mind is loosened.
Breathing out, we enjoy the fresh open field of our mind.

HUMILITY CLEARS THE WAY

My eyes wide open,
I see the tangle of my mind reflected in nature.
With humility
I clear the way.

When dealing with the tangle of our garden, the mindful practice of humility is one of the most valuable tools we can have. Humility makes us vulnerable despite our instinct to shield ourselves. It makes us softer. In dealing with tenacious weeds, soft is good. Pulling too hard on the perceived intruder will break its green growth at the soil's line, leaving the root to quickly reestablish itself upon our departure. With humility and softness, we learn how to address the coarse or fine nature of our weedy companions. We enter a relationship with our garden, with our weeds, and with ourselves.

When we turn toward the things in our garden that repel us, we turn toward those tangles in ourselves that we often neglect and ignore. We look mindfully to see if the roots spread out, or if they go deep. Our garden's weeds show us where we are stuck and where we hold on too tightly in our lives. As we begin to truly see the tangle of our mind reflected in our garden, our grasp becomes wise and compassionate. With humility we begin to clear the way.

My eyes wide open,
True gardening takes courage. Breathing in, we resolve to enter our garden with our eyes open. We enter the tangle that is at once our garden and ourselves.

I see the tangle of my mind reflected in nature.
Breathing out, realizing, as within, so without—we turn towards the tangle of our garden resolved to understand ourselves more deeply.

With humility
Breathing in, we allow humility to inspire openness, vulnerability, and authenticity in our gardening.

I clear the way.
Breathing out, we release our resistance.

THE WISDOM OF WEEDS

Knowing weeds are valuable allies,
I listen closely to their truth.
With understanding and compassion,
I embrace their wisdom as my own.

Weeds are wise. They know how to survive in the most grueling conditions. Even without water they tenaciously take up as much space as they are given.

They'll take over our entire garden if we do not curb their appetite for nutrients and land. Weeds can seem like intruders thwarting our well-thought-out plans and vision. But their tenacious presence, and how we deal with them, can point us to many insights about the more aggressive emotions of our inner landscape. Seeds of anger, greed, and hatred sow themselves into the fabric of our consciousness like the thistle, oxalis, and dandelions are sown into the soil of our garden.

If our weeds are not tended, they have the capacity to proliferate exponentially through our thoughts, words, and actions. Our weeds cause us to suffer, and if we lack awareness, their seeds may be cast widely upon the wind allowing our weeds, in the form of suffering and harm, to grow in other people's gardens as well. The more we know about our weeds—the more we learn how to embrace their messages—the better prepared we are to take care of our garden and ourselves.

Weeds indicate the places in our garden that we have neglected, the places where the soil has not been turned, and life has not been tended. When we struggle with emotions such as anger, we can glean from the whispers and thorns of our weed friends that there is a place within us that has not been nurtured. Often lying below our anger is grief or sadness. In much the same way as we embrace the tangle of weeds in our garden with a firm but tender grip, we can turn toward our anger, touch it sincerely, understand it, and know the truth of it. As we water the seeds of understanding and compassion within us, our anger is alleviated and our inner garden is restored to its innate, always present wholeness.

Knowing weeds are valuable allies,
Breathing in, we know that weeds are the gateway to deep understanding and compassion.

I listen closely to their truth.
Breathing out, we let our weeds water the seeds of insight within us.

With understanding and compassion,
Breathing in, we allow compassion to grow wherever we find ourselves.

I embrace their wisdom as my own.
Breathing out, spending time immersed in the language of our weeds, their wisdom finds a place to live in our being.

THE POINT OF PRUNING

When I prune
I remove the old.
In its place
new life grows.

Pruning can seem an overwhelming task, especially when we are standing face-to-face with a Cecil Brunner rose. Its thorns thick with age, and its canes arching wildly over the neighbor's eight-foot fence and onto his garage, we can choose to see the rose as a formidable obstacle that needs to be tamed, or as a great opportunity to make real space in our garden and ourselves—not to mention as an opportunity to make peace with our neighbor who has long tolerated our unruly rose climbing in his yard.

The trepidation of facing the thorns of the Cecil Brunner can be lessened if we understand why we are pruning it. Understanding the rose will only bloom on new growth gives our pruning real purpose. Wanting her to bloom radiantly, we address Cecil Brunner's over-grown branches, not hesitating to really prune them hard into their heavy old wood. We bend and move slowly and mindfully in accordance with the direction and placement of the rose's thorns and riley canes to avoid getting completely entangled in them as we work. Bravely pruning into the rose's old growth gives it the chance to bloom magnificently again in the spring—nature's reward for our mindful labors.

Pruning is a process of removing the old so that the new can have a space to grow and bloom. Courage is needed as we let go of the old and known for the new and unknown. Once again, our garden can be a wonderful mirror of our inner emotional terrain. Are there thought processes, habitual actions, or stories we tell ourselves that are just not viable, healthy, or true anymore? Do we hold on to old behaviors and ways of being that no longer serve us? This is our very own old growth, accumulated over many years. Mindfully pruning the Cecil Brunner in our garden, we can prune away the old stuck patterns inside of ourselves as well, opening space for the sprouts of new qualities such as clarity, peace, and calmness to grow and take root within our being.

Our stories—the inner turmoil that happens in our minds when we do not understand the true nature of a situation—are like the thorns of the rose. The more we move around inside the thoughts of our story, the more we get caught up on their edges and thorns. If we continue in this way for long, movement by movement our sweatshirt, that was meant to protect us, gets tangled up in the old growth of our preconceived ideas. Hardly able to move, we miss the present moment all together. With our mindfulness, however, we can prune our attention away from our stories. Bravely pruning hard into our old growth, we can remove the old canes and thorns of our wrong perceptions and misunderstanding, opening ourselves to the vast space of the present reality. Free of the tenacious grasp of our stories, we can fill ourselves with the freshness of the moment, and our new growth will bring us the beautiful flowers of peace and clarity.

When I prune
Breathing in, we vow to prune mindfully, understanding that our pruning makes space inside our garden and

ourselves for peace and clarity.

I remove the old.
We must risk the removal of the old in order to stimulate new growth. This is true of our garden as well as of ourselves. Breathing out, we resolve to remove the old with courage.

In its place
Pruning into the old growth of our garden and ourselves we make space for new life, growth, and blooms. Breathing in, we enjoy the process as we mindfully make room for the new.

new life grows.
Into the space once inhabited by the old growth of our roses and our wrong perceptions grow the qualities of clarity, calm, and peace. Breathing out, we are grateful for our courage to face letting go of the old in order to allow the new growth to bloom in the sanctuary of our garden and our soul.

PEACE IS MY SIGNPOST

In the clearing of my garden,
The tangle of my mind is loosened.
Peace and joy are my signposts.

I am on the right path.

Learning to embrace our interior and exterior tangle is an arduous task. However, the space we clear allows for our wisdom and understanding to bloom into the beautiful lotus of inner peace and joy. In the clearing of our weeds, our mind clears. We find ourselves more at ease. Peace and joy are the signposts letting us know we are on the right path.

In the clearing of my garden,
Breathing in, the open simplicity of the land quiets our mind.

The tangle of my mind is loosened.
Breathing out, the tangle of our mind is released into the air of our garden, and we relax. Garden and gardener rest peacefully within each other's embrace.

Peace and joy are my signposts.
Breathing in, we are in harmony with nature, and the seeds of peace and joy are watered within us.

I am on the right path.
Breathing out, we acknowledge the wisdom of our inner peace and joy as they guide us in bringing the vision for our garden to life.

chapter 5

THE HEART OF THE GARDEN

Touching the Earth's skin
with all my senses,
I get to know the heart of my garden,
and I vow to nurture it.

Our dedicated weeding has cleared the earth, opening it to life's potential. Now we can see the soil we are working. Soil is the heart of our garden, sending sunlight, rainwater, oxygen, and nutrients to all of our garden's inhabitants just as the human heart supplies oxygen and nutrients to our bodies. To understand the heart of our garden, we need to study the delicate, ever-changing conditions of its soil.

The fertility of our soil depends on our ability to look below the surface of things, to see the richness of life found at the bottom of death and decay. It depends on our ability to turn toward the deflated, limp slime and slurry that is called compost. Buried in the death folds of aged horse dung, last week's butternut squash soup, and yesterday's burnt toast, lies the fuel of our garden's growth.

In our compost pile, growth and decay give birth to each other. Their balance sustains our garden. Composting—engaging in the process of life falling apart and coming back together in new combinations and forms—is the gardener's gift to the earth, and the earth's gift to the gardener. Both are richer for having entered into relationship with one another.

Touching the Earth's skin
Breathing in, we hold the earth in our hands.

with all my senses,
Breathing out, we touch the life of our soil. With our eyes, our nose, and our hands we feel into the earth, we

assess it. Mindfully we take note, and we keep ourselves
open to what we find.

I get to know the heart of my garden,
Breathing in, we listen to the heart of our garden—its
soil—and we discern its health and well-being.

and I vow to nurture it.
Breathing out, we commit to taking care of the land
and the soil. Together, garden and gardener grow rich.

FULL CIRCLE COMPOST

Compost expresses as a circle.
Life begets death begets life.
I look deeply into the mounds of decay,
and see life living in its fold.

Deep in our compost pile, the never-ending cycle of
life and death takes place at an accelerated rate. In the
mounding up of layers of raw leftovers and dead leaves,
we find life embedded within the rich, fertile rot of
our compost. Living in the darkness at the bottom
of our compost, microscopic organisms consume the
skulls and hulls of our last garden and transform them
into new life.

There, lying in the belly of our compost, is an

opportunity to take a sincere look at the impermanence of all things. Nature is impermanence in action. It knows the unspoken richness found living in the mouth of decay. Death—the fecundity of rot—is nature's muse, beckoning new life into the smelly lair of its decomposing layers. We can learn from nature's contentment with death and dying, and begin to see death as simply a part of life, as we witness our compost pile. Taking to heart what we learn from our garden's compost, our relationship with death shifts, we soften like the rich, ebony of decomposed organic matter living at the bottom of our compost pile, and we, too, become rich. Seeing our compost with the eye of mindfulness, we have the insight to see life follows death in an unending circle. In the light of our understanding the fear of death loosens its grip on us.

Compost expresses as a circle.
Breathing in, we accept the circle of life and death our compost embodies, and we become its heartfelt caregiver. With our in-breath we open ourselves to the impermanence of all things, and we befriend death as a natural part of living.

Life begets death begets life.
Breathing out, we know that life falls apart into death and decay only to recombine into life again. Knowing this, we can turn the soil of our ripe horse manure as comfortably as we tend the soil beneath our favorite butterfly bush.

I look deeply into the mounds of decay,
Breathing in, we, as gardeners of the heart, have the courage to look deeply into the mounds of decay that constitute our compost pile, to breathe in their putrid breath as our own, and to smile at the possibilities of life living in their slurry. Happily, we join the great round of nature.

and see life living in its fold.
As we embrace death as the harbinger of new life, our fear of death loosens its grip on us. Breathing out, we sigh with relief.

HONING HUMUS

Honing humus,
I honor its rich culture.
I offer its wild fertility
to the soil of my garden.

Humus is the stuff of which compost dies to become. It is the rich, dark, ebony-hued stream of decomposed organic matter living at the bottom of our compost pile. Humus is a vastly complex culture that feeds on itself to create new life. So rich is it in nature we must give it respect and room to grow.

It takes dedicated piling and turning for our smoldering hot compost pile to transform into the black gold culture of humus. When we offer this culture to our soil, it is forever changed. The nature and fertility of humus gives the soil greater ability to absorb nutrients and retain water. It balances our soil's pH at about 6.0–6.8, the perfect acidity for plant growth, and it increases our soil's ability to absorb and immobilize toxic heavy metals, keeping our plants safe from their harmful effects. In the absence of toxic heavy metals, the natural microorganisms and healthy ecology of our soil is capable of reestablishing itself and sustaining life.

Honing humus,
Breathing in with humility, we build and turn the death and decay of our compost into humus, the ebony gold of its birthright.

I honor its rich culture.
Breathing out, we honor and acknowledge the vast, rich, and complex culture of our humus as we recognize the wisdom buried in the folds of its darkness.

I offer its wild fertility
Never constituted from the same ingredients, humus is wild in its fertility. Breathing in, we offer its wild fertility to our overly domesticated soil.

to the soil of my garden.
Breathing out, we allow the culture of humus to spread out across our land. Its undomesticated life force radiates

out into our plants, into our bodies, and into our lives.

DIRT POOR TO FILTHY RICH

Hidden in my compost
is a buried treasure.
Immeasurable in its value,
to my garden it is black gold.

Taking up very little space (I recommend no bigger than approximately three cubic feet), our compost pile is a powerhouse of nutrients, nutrient storage, and water supply. Each pile has its own unique character and personality formed by the ingredients that make up its constitution: whispering of rotten eggs, fallen persimmons, redwood needles, and old love letters yellowed with time. These ingredients marinate together, forming infinite relationships that never existed before, and give each mound its own enchanting, molten mojo.

It takes mindfulness to understand the ripeness and potency of our compost, as well as the needs of our garden. Our compost is ripe and ready when it is cool, and allows for critters like manure worms, pill bugs, and centipedes—which cannot handle the heat of immature compost—to inhabit its rich brown hills. The pile's scent also changes from the putrid smell of decomposition to one that is sweet and woodsy like fresh earth. Each year, once our compost is cool and ripe, we can add approximately two inches of its richness to our garden's soil.

Sharing the wealth of our compost with our garden's soil transforms both our garden's fertility, and it changes us. Mindfully recognizing the vast richness of the soil right beneath our feet—soil we helped to create—can help us transform feelings of scarcity into feelings of gratitude. When we find ourselves concerned that we do not have enough either materially or emotionally, we can turn to the deep, ebony richness of our garden's soil, and smile, knowing we are rich beyond measure. Living in the earth just beneath our feet is life's infinite potential.

Land that once stood fallow and empty is now prime real estate for flora and fauna—for all life—to thrive and grow. Dirt poor to filthy rich, our garden now has the pure potential of supporting life itself. The ripe wealth of death's arrival in our garden as we apply our compost to the blank canvas of the soil's open space, beckon all life to its fold. We, with humus on the palms of our hands and the bottom of our boots, are the wealthiest gardeners of all.

Hidden in my compost

Looking deeply into our compost pile, we see the wealth of nutrients available to share with the flora and fauna of our garden. Breathing in, we gladly accept its offering.

is a buried treasure.

Breathing out, we express our gratitude for having discovered the buried treasure of our compost's vast richness—a complex fortune of unfathomed relationships joining to form the ebony-black humus of our garden.

Immeasurable in its value,

Breathing in, we offer the wealth of our compost to the fabric of our soil. The seeming emptiness of death exudes life's pure potential right before our eyes, allowing our garden to thrive. Breathing in, we humbly offer the wealth of our compost to the fabric of our soil. In our offering, the emptiness of death that holds life's pure potential becomes a priceless jewel when placed upon the earth.

to my garden it is black gold.

With compost as its nutriment, our soil now has the capacity to transmute rain, sun, and nutrients into the life forms of roses, apples, and rhubarb. Breathing out, we know garden and gardener are wealthy beyond measure.

chapter 6

SOWING THE SEEDS

The earth lies beneath me,
a wide open canvas.
Into it I sow
the seeds of my mindfulness.

The soil of our garden is the canvas upon which we paint life. What we paint, the final product, is inconsequential. It is the quality of our heart, and our presence while we are painting, that matters. Growing a garden, just as cultivating our true nature, requires mindfulness. Gardening and spiritual practice have within their embodiment the fundamental essence of returning us to the source.

When we garden, we partake in an ancient ritual. What we give our attention to is what grows—literally and figuratively. The seeds we sow and nurture today become the fruits we reap tomorrow. We chose to nurture happiness or sorrow, contentment or desire, and anger or love.

The digging and pulling, the watering and weeding, the planting and fertilizing of our garden, when done with mindfulness, offer us an opportunity to plant and water the seeds we wish to flourish in our lives and our garden. When we recite a gatha with one hundred percent of our being while we garden, body and mind as one, the vibration of our speech carries true power—the power of transformation. Gardening mindfully, the land and our consciousness are transformed, and we, and our garden, blossom into beautiful flowers.

The earth lies beneath me,

Aware of the earth beneath our feet, we touch the source of all life. Breathing in, we water the seeds of love, compassion, and joy present within us. We are happy to be alive walking on the earth.

a wide open canvas.

Our land and our consciousness are wide open fields awaiting our creative expression. Breathing out, we allow nature to unfold.

Into it I sow

As gardeners we are also artists. The quality and focus of our attention sow the beauty of our heart into the soil of our garden. It is the quality of the heart that matters, and not how straight we can plant a row of corn.

Breathing in, we embody the expansiveness of the sky, and we sow our seeds with mindfulness into the earth and into our consciousness.

the seeds of my mindfulness.

The most precious offering we can give to life is our presence. Breathing out, we become present, watering the seeds of our mindfulness practice while we garden. Deeply rooted in the present moment, we allow nature's wisdom to unfold without attachment.

DIGGING DOWN

I entrust myself to my garden.
My garden entrusts herself to me.
Digging down reverently, I offer these words,
"Dear Earth, I am here for you."

Garden and gardener grow together like the marriage between a climbing red rose and a brilliant purple clematis sharing the same arbor. We have spent time getting to know our land, we have cleared a space, and now we are ready to plant the seeds of our mindfulness into the soil. We bring our bodies and our minds to our planting in the garden. We are present.

Within us, live the patterns of the sky, the flow of the winds, and the innate character and movement of our environment. Our understanding forges the metal of our spades and the flesh of our hands with the land's wisdom. Mindfully placing our spade into the earth, digging down, we can say, "Dear Earth, I am here for you—truly here." These words acknowledge our honoring of the Earth and all it does to sustain our lives. With our hands on the smooth wooden handle of our spade, we give our body's energy and life force to the soil, and we offer the land a breath of air as we open it to the sky. Through the alignment of our thoughts, words, and actions with the natural world, we begin to plant the seeds of our mindfulness with love.

I entrust myself to my garden.
When we spend time in our garden we come to know its ways and its truth—the direction and force of the season's winds, the movement of light and shadow, and the temperament of the soil itself through the inhabitants it allows or denies. Breathing in, we entrust ourselves to the wisdom of nature and allow it to inform our actions.

My garden entrusts herself to me.
Lying beneath our feet, the Earth entrusts her care to us. Mindfully, we have cleared a space with our weeding, we have cultivated good heart in our soil with our compost, and we now excavate the soil to receive the seeds of our garden's newest flora. Breathing out, we open the soil of our garden mindfully as we honor the

land and all its inhabitants.

Digging down reverently, I offer these words,
Earth, air, water, fire—these are the threads that weave us into the fabric of life—to the earth worm and the dragon fly, to the red-tailed hawk and the garter snake. Breathing in, we vow to dig down reverently into the earth careful to preserve all life living in its folds.

"Dear Earth, I am here for you."
With these words we give our full presence to the Earth. We express true love, as we compassionately excavate the soil while offering our most prized possession, our presence. Garden and gardener intertwine in the soil of mindful awareness, and both thrive. Breathing out, we are present to the Earth.

DRINKING IN JOY

Breathing mindfully,
I dip the cup of my awareness
into the wellspring of the here and now.
I drink from the joy of the present moment.

Following our breath while we plant heightens all our senses. When we listen to the chicadee's voice, look at the potential in the subtly-hued seeds we hold in our hands, and press our fingers into the soil's rich mineral-filled texture, we come to know the reality of our physical world and surroundings, and this deep knowledge can bring joy.

Our happiness and suffering are intimately connected to the health and well-being of our garden and the world. With this knowledge, we become more aware of the potential for joy always around us.

Our conscious breathing is the vehicle by which we continually return to the present moment. Planting seeds in rhythm with our breath guides us into the here and now where life lives. Joining the life-giving ground of the present moment we plant and water the seeds of joy, peace, and understanding in ourselves. Our joy and happiness nourish our garden, ourselves, and our world. Our joy nourishes our practice and deepens our connection with all of life.

Breathing mindfully,
Breathing in, I feel the joy of the present moment. Life is happening all around me.

I dip the cup of my awareness
Breathing out, all my senses are alive to the wonder of the earth. I know each seed contains the whole universe.

into the wellspring of the here and now.
Breathing in, aware of the possibilities in each seed, I allow my cup to be filled with now.

I drink from the joy of the present moment.
Breathing out, I release a seed, trusting in the earth to do its work, and move to the next. There is no need for clinging or worry.

CULTIVATING COMPASSION

Kindness is my true nature.
When I acknowledge my interconnection
with all beings, animals, plants, and minerals,
I cultivate compassion.

Compassion is natural, but it takes courage. Our compassion is awakened when we allow our heart to soften toward our world, our garden, and ourselves. When we look at our world with the eyes of our heart, we can see how all of life is interconnected. Looking deeply at a pomegranate from our garden, we can see it is made up of many nonpomegranate elements—sky, sun, clouds, rain, earth, and minerals. All of these elements are required if the pomegranate is to grow. Without them, there is no pomegranate.

The pomegranate's sweet fruit provides energy for our bodies. It becomes a part of us. Its nourishment offers energy, allowing us to think, to speak, and to act. The pomegranate continues on inside of us. And as our thoughts, words, and actions touch the lives of many other beings, animals, plants, and minerals, the rich, vibrant, red juice of the pomegranate lives on in all of these elements, too. Our human bodies are completely connected with the body of the Earth, and all other beings.

The minerals of the earth make up our bodies as well as the beauty around us. Rain becomes our rivers, our tea, and our blood. The sun activates photosynthesis in the leaves of trees so they may grow, and it offers vitamin D to our bodies, assisting us in absorbing calcium. The sky feeds the forests with carbon dioxide, and we breathe oxygen from the trees. Minerals, water, sun, and air constitute our bodies' flesh, muscles, and bones. The more conscious we are of this shared life, the more compassion is sown within us, drawing the kindness of our true nature into action.

Kindness is my true nature.

When we open ourselves to embrace the truth of our interconnectedness with all beings, animals, plants, and minerals, a quivering compassion arises from the ground of our being. Turning toward life as an extension of ourselves, breathing in, our thoughts, words, and actions are inspired by the kindness of our true nature.

When I acknowledge my interconnection

Having the courage to let down the armor of our self-protection and preservation, we come to see our world with the eyes of the heart, and our interbeing with all of life reveals itself to us. As the pomegranate is made of nonpomegranate elements, we, too, are made of non-human elements—air, fire, earth, and water. All of life is made of the same elements uniting it into a single whole. With our out-breath, we acknowledge our oneness with all of life.

with all beings, animals, plants, and minerals,

All of the elements in our garden are intertwined with the sun, the rain, the earthworms, and the sweat of the first gardeners from whom we learned how to garden. Minerals to bone, water to blood, sky to breath, breathing in, with our fresh in-breath, we take it all in, and we honor the source and circle of this one life we are all living. Acknowledging our oneness, we water the seed of compassion in our consciousness.

I cultivate compassion.

When we truly see how directly our lives are interdependent with the sun, the soil, and the earthworm—with all of life—compassion is cultivated within us, and we are naturally inclined to give our care, attention, and nurturance to the life surrounding and dwelling in us. Our understanding grants us the insight to see that together we share a common destiny. Breathing out, we sow the seeds of our compassion and kindness into the soil of our garden.

WHEN SEEDS DON'T GROW

Sometimes, even with mindfulness,
my garden fails to thrive.
With breath, mind, and hands free,
the seed of my equanimity emerges.

Gardening is a great exploration and adventure, and no matter how thoughtful and careful we may be, it is unavoidable that some aspects of our vision and dream for our land will not thrive. Our failures often tell more about ourselves than any success ever will. The ego, cunning as it is, can gracefully disguise itself as even-mindedness in the sugary sweet praise that lies in the wake of our success; however, the depth and truth of who we really are reveals itself perhaps more in our response to our challenges.

Obstacles and challenges in our gardening keep us humble. They are good medicine helping us to become more authentic. When taken in the proper way, challenges can snap us back to our senses. Learning—specifically, learning from adverse conditions—keeps us alive, growing. And it keeps us real.

When the blue beets we planted in our garden do not take root, we learn something about our beets and ourselves. How we respond to the challenges of our garden teaches us about ourselves. Do we meet the perceived failure with animosity, or do we turn to the situation with compassion, and ask for greater insight, understanding, and patience as to why our beets did not grow? Can we take a step back? Can we see with the eyes of dispassion, and simply note what is without having to find blame or pointing our finger—not even at ourselves?

When we slow down and coordinate our breath with our observations regarding the life of our garden—or the lack thereof—we experience a little bit of distance, a little breathing room around the situation. In the space of this breath our mind frees up, and our ego loses its grip on us. We come to understand that how we respond to the situation is more important than the situation itself, and it is our choice how we respond. Our reaction and the focus of our attention are really all we ever have control over in any situation. Resting in just what is, without rendering it as good or bad, opens us to possibility, and leaves the palette of our mind free to receive what our garden is telling us about its soil, water, sun, and plants. Garden and gardener deepen in their witnessing and knowing of one another.

Sometimes, even with mindfulness,
Breathing in, we are aware that it is our intention to give our full awareness to our gardening, and to let go of the fruits of our labor. This is our sincere offering as we breathe.

my garden fails to thrive.
Seeing failure as way of understanding our garden and ourselves more deeply, breathing out, we release any temptation to blame or find fault.

With breath, mind, and hands free,
Breath full, hands empty, and mind open, we breathe in life's unpredictability. Breathing out, we stay open, flexible, and soft.

the seed of my equanimity emerges.
In the soft soil of our openness and flexibility, the seed of equanimity emerges. Breathing out, we share our even-mindedness with the Earth and all its beings.

chapter 7

WATER'S WISDOM

Ancient in your wisdom,
Water, teach me
flexibility, persistence, and impermanence,
that I may know true power.

WATER, OUR TEACHER

The water we drink today has quenched the thirst of many mouths before ours. From cloud to rain, to stream, to well, to plant and body, to air, and back to cloud, for millions of years, water has traveled from sky to sea and back again. Our physical bodies are approximately sixty percent water. Every cell of our body carries water's presence and life-giving nourishment. To say we are connected to the rain, the snow, and the fog is a bit of an understatement.

Watching how water moves and flows across and into our garden's soil returns us to the underground truth of ourselves. Water easily changes from solid ice, cooling our drink, to the drinking water itself, to the steam billowing from the tea in our cup. Its nature is fluid and constantly changing. In our mindful observance of water's nonresistance and flexibility to change, we can learn to be more supple and spontaneous, going with the flow of life.

Water doesn't just change its own shape; it also possesses the ability to change the shape of the land. Glaciers of ice and rocks have carved the canyons and formed the mountains of our Earth over thousands of years. Inch by inch, millimeter by millimeter, water teaches us the power of flexibility, persistence, and impermanence.

We can witness these same characteristics of malleability, staying power, and change in the force of the sea's unending waves crashing upon the rocky crags of the shoreline, slowly wearing away its sharp edges, and in time erasing their forms altogether. Because our bodies are predominantly water themselves, we can resonate deeply with its steady force and rhythm. We can learn to harness water's persistence within ourselves, focusing our attention and vital force mindfully on our beneficial goals and visions for our garden, for our lives, and for the world.

When we discover a root from a neighboring tree in the exact position we had wished to plant our azalea, we can embody water's flexibility. Going with the flow, we allow another location to reveal itself to us without holding tenaciously to our plan. We see water's persistence in us as we remain committed to our mindfulness practice as we clear our garden's relentless weeds.

The living force of water also invites us to acknowledge life's impermanence. We witness water's fearless embodiment of change in the destruction of entire villages lying in the path of a hungry tsunami. Instantly, a life we may have clung to disappears under the violent thrashing waves.

Once our hearts have settled from such a disaster and loss, we can turn toward the water's fierce movement and begin to see it as an invitation to let go and make a fresh start. Huddling close to those who have survived the storm with us, the power of water helps us recognize the things in life we most deeply value— relationships, contact, and community. As we begin to put our lives together again, we have changed. Due to the stripping of the water's rampage, we are much more aware of our interbeing with all beings, animals, plants, and minerals, and the frailty of life. We grow in our compassion as we gain an understanding of the tender vulnerability of life. Water teaches us to live closely with the truth of our impermanence.

With water as our teacher, we learn flexibility, perseverance, and the truth of our impermanence. As we embody these qualities, we learn to live with true power, and the ancient wisdom of water is alive in us.

Ancient in your wisdom,
Breathing in, we honor the ancient wisdom of water— its travels, its embodiment of truth, and the way it teaches us flexibility, perseverance, and impermanence.

Water, teach me
As we water our garden we give our mindful attention to the water's wisdom. Breathing out, we release our attachments and witness the water's skillful movement across, and into, the soil of our garden.

flexibility, persistence, and impermanence,
Breathing in, we drink in water's embodiment of flexibility, persistence, and impermanence as we water our garden. Water is wise; we embody its wisdom through our mindful gardening.

that I may know true power.

The qualities of water teach us to trust and enjoy life's spontaneous unfolding with steadiness and grace. Breathing out, we know the freedom of living in and from our true power as we discover that we and our garden are life's creative, ever-evolving unfoldment.

HAND AND HOE

Don't think you will die of thirst, dear soil.
I bring to you the sky and the sea.
I carry it to you in my hands,
and together we shall drink.

Watering is an opportunity to become present. Becoming aware of the merged drops of water's arched form as they touch the Earth's skin and enter its pores returns us to the softness of life. If we look closely, we may catch a glimpse of the rainbow dancing on its fluid form—a dynamic, liquid hologram—right before our eyes. Actively observing as we water by hand has a soothing effect on the mind. Watching the drops of water in their journey to our garden's soil slows us down and brings us to the Earth's nourishing surface. It is good for the soil and the soul to hand water our garden at least once a week. Hand watering grounds us. The Earth being our home, we can gain deep comfort from the weekly ritual of hand watering its soil.

Water and gardener—comrades in softening and nourishing the soil—have another ally in their quest to care for the Earth and its soil: a simple tool called a hoe. Hand-in-hand, hose and hoe ensure that our watering practices preserve the water-absorbing softness of the Earth's skin. Watering by hand, and loosening the soil with a hoe, ensures the life of our soil and its ability to drink deeply from the water we offer it.

Don't think you will die of thirst, dear soil.
Breathing in, we enter fully into a relationship with our soil, a relationship rooted in love and compassion for all living things.

I bring to you the sky and the sea.
Breathing out, we acknowledge our connection with all of life. We recognize that the water we offer has been gifted to us by the sky and the sea. Our offering is humble and wise.

I carry it to you in my hands,
Bringing water to our soil by hand expresses our devotion to the Earth's well-being, and our willingness to be fully engaged in relationship with our garden. Through our intention and hand rendering, the water we offer carries our heart's signature into the land. Heart of garden and heart of gardener merge with this in-breath.

and together we shall drink.

In solidarity, garden and gardener drink the life-giving water of the sky and the sea. Breathing out, our thirst is quenched.

WATERING WISELY

Let me listen closely
to the language of water's movement.
May it inform my practice,
that I may water wisely.

How do we learn to water our gardens wisely? We learn from those who have walked the land before us, those who survived droughts and floods. We read books about our plants and their moisture require-ments, and we learn about the character of our soil as best we can. However, when it comes right down to it, learning to water our soil just enough for our gar-den's inhabitants to thrive without drowning, we need to allow ourselves the time to become intimate with water itself—its movement, its speed, its direction—specifically, as it relates and interacts with our soil. No matter what we learn from books, our garden, and spe-cifically our soil itself, in all of its quirky wildness, will be our best teacher.

In understanding the nature of our soil it is helpful to

observe water's movement across and into its rich brown pores. Is it fast, or is it slow? Does it meander for a while before it seeps down, or does it slither quickly into the soil like a frightened king snake with curious humans fast on its tail? We learn the language of water's presence, using words like: drought, dust, wilt, trickle, deluge, rain, frost, snow, drizzle, mist, fog, turgor pressure, drooping, flagging, soggy, muddy, sloppy, precipitation, absorption, transpiration, evaporation, and condensation.

Watching water's movement with an open curiosity, we aim to allow our watering practice to find the middle ground between watering too much or too little. Alan Chadwick, a wise gardener and author, encourages us to understand our soil's temperament and ability to absorb water with this maxim, "Water so that the soil can dry out."[4]

These are wise words, and we can only know their application to our garden by being in very close relationship with our soil. Faces close to the earth, our real job in learning to water wisely is to listen to and be a steady observer of water's movement into our soil. Watering practice is mindfulness practice. Remaining the ever-mindful witness of our watering allows our responses to the soil and weather conditions to remain supple and spontaneous like water itself. Watering mindfully we assure our garden's ability to adapt and thrive in the

4   Quoted in Wendy Johnson, *Gardening at the Dragon's Gate: At Work in the Wild and Cultivated World* (New York: Bantam Dell A Division of Random House, Inc., 2008), 169.

ever-changing conditions of the natural world.

Let me listen closely

Inhaling deeply, we vow to lean into the wisdom of our garden by giving it our full attention. Listening closely to the water's flow, the wind's direction, and the sun's angle we learn the conditions of our land and its inhabitants. We draw this wisdom into our mindfulness practice of watering.

to the language of water's movement.

Breathing out, we breathe the breath of the wind. Humbly we speak water's language as best we can as we mindfully model its natural flow.

May it inform my practice,

Breathing in, we allow the wisdom of the natural world to inform our watering as a mindfulness practice. Observing the ever-changing conditions of our garden's soil—from bone dry to saturated—we practice beginner's mind, staying open and receptive to the earth's needs. We listen closely, and allow our practice to be guided by our observations.

that I may water wisely.

Supple and fluid like water itself, our practice follows the flow of water's natural course, responding to each swale and slope with skill. Breathing out, we offer water's life to our soil wisely, watering so that the soil can dry out again. Our mindful practice keeps us in nature's flow and grace.

SINGING IN THE RAIN

Dear garden, I am in love.
Singing in your downpour,
my voice joyfully joins
the voice of the rain.

Moving mindfully to the flow of nature, we are sure to fall in love with watering our garden. One delightful way we can celebrate water is to experience and enjoy the rain directly. Walking in the tip-tapping raindrops of a downpour, we immerse ourselves in the water's voice. Singing as we walk, our voice merges with the voice of the rainfall, and the patterns of water coursing down the channeled bark of a redwood tree become close and intimate like the blood carried in our veins. Giving our heart to water, we fall in love, and the rain falls to meet us.

Whenever we give our attention and heart to nature we are met in that field, wherever we stand—whether it is in our garden, in the shower, in a swimming pool, or taking a sip of water. We can enjoy communing with the water of our garden while we shower, imagining we are a tree during a soft summer rain. What does it feel like to have the water slowly course down our limbs? Is this what it feels like to be a tree? In our swimming pool we can imagine we are a lotus flower floating on the calm clear surface of a pond. Feeling ourselves held by the water, we can experience the life of a beautiful lotus. Even in taking a simple drink of water through a straw, we can join our awareness and our hearts with water and with our garden, as we imagine being an iridescent ruby-throated humming bird sipping water off the surface of a nasturtium leaf. Wherever and whenever we are mindful of water, we join its voice.

Dear garden, I am in love.
Spending time in our garden, experiencing and drinking in the same waters, we enter into a deep, and sincere relationship with nature. Breathing in, we declare our love and devotion for our garden.

Singing in your downpour,
Breathing out, we offer our voice to the rain-filled sky.

my voice joyfully joins
Voices joined, soil and soul drenched, our song is filled with the wild music of our true nature. Water to water, human voice to nature's voice, we breathe in delight while we sing.

the voice of the rain.
Breathing out with untethered abandon, our voice one of the many raindrops free-falling in a tip-tapping parade to the Earth, we nourish the heart and soul of garden and gardener.

chapter 8

SHARING
SPACE

A lotus to you
my garden's guest.
To you, a bodhisattva,
I vow to be.

Our garden is not ours alone, even if it is in our own tiny backyard. Animals, insects, and fungi share it with us. The guests in our garden can teach us such things as reverence for life, nonattachment to views, and generosity, if we stay open. Committing ourselves to mindful awareness in the face of all the fangs, claws, stingers, slime, and drool is not always an easy task, but is worthy of our attention and practice. With our commitment we vow to grow.

I invite us to look with the eyes of understanding and insight to see that all creatures in our garden are our guests. Just as we give attention to our interactions with friends who arrive in our home, we need to pay close attention to how we treat our outdoor guests as well. Admittedly, some guests feel more welcome than others. It is easy to feel close and accommodating to those who leave a gentle footprint in our garden. They are our friends. Butterflies, ladybugs, and nighttime cicadas are a few of the guests that tread lightly in our sanctuary. They conjure sweet memories with their delightful hovering and calming rhythms. Our relationship with them is joyful and tender, and we naturally feel a desire to protect their lives. They reflect the calmness, grace, and gentleness we seek in ourselves. We are comfortable with these qualities and find joy in the presence of our visitors that evoke them in us. As they arrive upon our garden's threshold, we welcome them in as guests in our sanctuary.

Other guests are less easily welcome: from gophers, skunks, and raccoons; to cucumber beetles and cabbage loopers; to snails and slugs. They move upon our land with a heavier tread, leaving destruction in their wake. Due to the trail of wilted and slimy leaves, or the devastation of our beautiful chard and butter lettuce, often our initial response to these guests is one of repulsion; however, these unwelcome visitors can be our greatest teachers. They stretch us, taking us beyond our comfort zone.

Our seemingly unwelcome guests can inspire anger, fear, and greed in us, emotions that are also difficult or uncomfortable to welcome. These emotions, if not handled with awareness and tenderness, can leave huge footprints in the soil of our soul and our garden, destroying friendships, livelihood, and life. How do we deal with our less desirable external and internal guests? This is rich compost for us to touch with our mindfulness practice.

In our repulsion, we may want to immediately stomp the life out of our unwanted guests. Or we may prefer the more distant method of killing them with traps, thus keeping ourselves at arm's length from our thoughts and actions. It's good to acknowledge our desire to destroy our less desirable garden guests and emotions.

Our first response can be to pause and take a breath. Turning toward our unwanted guests with curiosity and openness—both the external and internal variety—we take time to learn about these visitors and get to know their habits and impacts on the life of our garden and our soul.

I have listened to many ways to do away with snails in the garden; from chemicals to getting them drunk on beer until they drown in their intoxicating host. A harmless, simple alternative to addressing our plant-devouring friends is to place copper in the form of stripping or pennies along the perimeter of our beloved planting beds. Copper is like Superman's kryptonite to snails, and they will naturally move away from it. With discernment and compassion we find a way for our unwanted guests to live without causing further harm to our sanctuary. We invite the seeds of our understanding, wisdom, and compassion into the same soil as that of our pesky guests—rodent, insect, disease, and emotions alike.

Learning how to interact with the unwanted guests of our outer landscape can teach us how to be with the thoughts, feelings, and habits of our inner landscape that impede our fullest loving expression. For example, turning toward a snail with compassion, giving it a peaceful alternative route leading away from our garden's flowers can teach us how to deal with our feelings of anger. Just as we did with our snail visitors, we first stop, breathe, and acknowledge anger's arrival in our emotional landscape. Our breath gives us time and space. It slows us down, brings us back to ourselves, and keeps us from saying or doing things we may later regret. Calmer now, taking a second and third breath, we turn toward our anger. We welcome it closer instead of pushing it away. With the same openness and curiosity we gave to the snail, we take time to learn about our anger: its felt-sense in our body, its source, and its request of us. Breathing mindfully, we inquire: Where is it located in our body? What is it trying to communicate to us?

Walking in our garden with our steps following the cadence of our breathing is a wonderful way to attune to our emotions and learn from them. A form of walking meditation, turning toward our emotions in this way gives us time to understand and gain insight about them. Just as we turn toward the rascally guests of our garden, we can do the same with our more difficult emotions, such as anger. We take time to get to know our anger, and we accept it as a part of us. Once we understand and respond to our anger, tenderly giving it our attention, we have an opportunity to choose how we express it. Just as we did with the snail, we give our anger an alternate route. We offer this new direction by beginning to cultivate anger's opposite—love. Understanding our anger—its source, needs, and request of us—leads us to having compassion for ourselves. Having compassion for ourselves is our first step in cultivating anger's opposite. We continue to cultivate love as we extend forgiveness and compassion to the perceived cause of our anger, allowing our insight to guide us. Looking deeply at the situation, we see the truth of it, and we are inspired to act with compassion and understanding just as we do with the snail. When we learn methods for dealing with the perceived intruders of our garden, it can teach us how to deal with our more difficult emotions.

A lotus to you

Breathing in, we see all beings, animals, plants, and minerals as precious; we offer our garden's inhabitants a lotus with our in-breath as a symbol of our good intentions.

my garden's guest.

Breathing out, we welcome all of our sanctuary's animals, insects, and diseases as our honored guests, and we vow to extend our curiosity and gentleness in learning how to share our sacred space with them.

To you, a bodhisattva,

A bodhisattva is a Buddhist term for a being who is committed to the care and liberation of all beings. The heart of a bodhisattva is that of a compassionate warrior. The bodhisattva knows how to hold a beautiful flower beyond the arc of discernment's sword, careful not to strike a fatal blow to its innocent life, while simultaneously wielding the action necessary for our garden's survival. Breathing in, we bring our best selves to our interactions with our garden's guests.

I vow to be.

Breathing out, we release our fear, judgment, and attachment to our views, allowing us to see more clearly. We think, speak, and act in our lives and our garden by seeing the precious opportunity of all life to cultivate our understanding and insight.

TOO SOON TO TELL

With awareness and curiosity
I grow from not knowing,
and the lotus of true understanding
blooms beautifully within me.

When we see things in our garden that frighten, alarm, or enrage us, we can stop, breathe, and observe, instead of reacting immediately. Patient curiosity is our friend. We pause and take a breath, and we learn to stay present with the more wily guests of our gardens and our minds.

Once the joy and excitement of designing and planting have passed, gardening can seem like hard work. Remaining in relationship with our gardens, and ourselves, takes courage and discipline, but it is a relationship that once entered and committed to brings us much joy. Just like any good relationship requires, we need to have the courage to let go of what we think we, and our garden, should be. Having found the temerity to stay present, we work, with our discipline to assist us, in continuously renouncing our point of view. Given time the lotus of understanding blooms inside of us as we gain insight into the nature of our gardens and ourselves. "No mud, no lotus," says Thich Nhat Hanh, a Buddhist monk, poet, and peace activist. A lotus needs mud to grow. We can think of our unwanted guests and emotions as "the mud." Through the mud, our genuine pursuit of staying present with mindfulness and curiosity allows "the lotus" of understanding to unfold beautifully within us.

With awareness and curiosity,
Breathing in, we explore how remaining aware and curious draws us into the details of life alive in the present moment. Living in the present moment, we take in life on life's terms, remaining open to just what is, and we enter an authentic relationship with our garden and ourselves.

I grow from not knowing,
Breathing out, when faced with a difficult emotion or a tough-skinned guest in our garden, breathing gives us space, and we know it may be too soon to tell what needs to be done. Our mindful breathing slows us down and allows us to be more comfortable with not knowing.

and the lotus of true understanding
Open-minded awareness helps us remain curious about the mysteries of life before us. Breathing in, we water the seeds of insight and true understanding in the soil of our being.

blooms beautifully within me.
Breathing out, grounded in the present moment, we can respond slowly and authentically to our garden's

perceived intruders and our difficult emotions, allowing the lotus of true understanding to bloom within us. Through our thoughts, words, and actions, we share its fragrance with the world.

FINDING COMMON GROUND

Garden and gardener are intertwined.
Two branches of the same vine,
we thrive
on common ground.

Finding common ground begins as early as the creative process and the design of our garden. Good design responds to the climate and topography of our land. It incorporates healthy cultured soil and disease- and drought-resistant native plants requiring lower maintenance. These are clear, simple measures we can take in encouraging the more damaging guests of our garden to live and thrive elsewhere.

Similarly, we can invest ourselves in cultivating a healthy environment for our inner landscape. We keep the soil of our physical form vital and strong by eating healthy foods, drinking good water, and getting rest. And we lower our susceptibility to sickness and disease by getting exercise that is compatible with our body and our lifestyle, and maintaining a positive outlook on life. Surrounding ourselves with healthy, spiritually-minded people, and a calm and peaceful environment, also assists us in our endeavors to stay healthy mentally.

Finding common ground with our garden requires great awareness and mindfulness. Despite our best efforts, sometimes we will cause harm with our gardening. The Zen gardener, Wendy Johnson, tells a story about a doe and her fawn having gotten trapped inside their garden. The gardeners tried to usher the deer toward the freedom of the coastal hills just beyond the garden's fence. True to their wild nature, however, once herded, the mother and fawn panicked. In her distress the mother deer threw herself against the fence which had been built expressly for keeping her safely out of the garden, and broke her neck. She died quickly under the tender observance of the gardeners. The fawn bounded silently back to freedom and was never seen again.

We need to find a way to garden without causing harm or taking life. Johnson says, "Gardener and pest are intertwined, made of each other. Practicing with this truth softens the edge between us."[5] As we allow the edge between ourselves and nature to soften, we grow in compassion. We see that we are all guests in the interconnected web of life, and we commit ourselves to finding common ground upon which all beings may thrive.

5   Wendy Johnson, *Gardening at the Dragon's Gate: At Work in the Wild and Cultivated World* (New York: Bantam Dell, 2008), 228.

Garden and gardener are intertwined.
Breathing in, we see our garden and ourselves as growing branches of the same vine.

Two branches of the same vine,
Intertwined as branches of a wisteria vine, the edge between garden and gardener softens into the patterns of the hills, the grasses, and the trees. We are they, and they are us. Breathing out, we breathe each other's breath.

we thrive
Compassion is born in the belly of our softening. Breathing in, we commit ourselves to slow down, to observe, to study, and to learn the ways of nature. With wisdom and mindfulness, we, our brother gopher, and our sister spider, find common ground upon which to live in harmony.

on common ground.
Breathing out, the air moves out of our lungs, and joins the air, the water, and the earth of our garden. Born and nurtured in the soil of our insight and understanding, we, and our garden grow on common ground, and all life thrives.

WHO IS HOME?

Knowing we are all guests,
I look with the eyes of my heart.
A compassionate warrior,
I honor all life.

Reverence for all life is a very helpful foundation as we begin to deal with our garden's guests. We need to ask, "Who is home?" And "Whose home is this?" Many of the animals, insects, and fungi we come across in our garden have lived on, in, and traveled through the dark veins of the Earth's soil long before we lay claim to the property's neatly defined borders. They are locals and this common ground—our garden—is land where we are all guests in each other's home.

One of the best ways to honor our shared inheritance of the Earth is by spending time getting to know our garden's vertebrates, invertebrates, and diseases. At ground zero of our garden's soil, we enter into direct relationship with all of them. Nose to snout, stinger, and spittle, we acknowledge and honor the perseverance and persistence of our garden's guests, whether they be four-, six-, or eight-legged; or squirmy, writhing, and legless. Mindful of our garden's locals, we learn to think like they behave, to notice their habits and patterns, and we try to understand their next move before they make it.

Dealing with the heavy tread of one of our garden's guests is not about control. It's about staying open and aware. We do our homework, we observe, and we take notes about their biting, chewing, and scratching. We seek to find the most harmonious and compassionate way to deal with our perceived intruders. Once we have acknowledged and become familiar with a pesky guest wreaking havoc on the life of our garden, we can discern just how much damage we, and our garden, can tolerate.

Consider the gopher. Gophers prefer to live in low coastal areas where the soil is soft and moist and supports good herbage production in the form of vegetation that has large, fleshy roots, bulbs, tubers, and other underground nutrient storage root systems. Sounds like our garden, right? It is. Watching the burrowing behavior of our gopher friends, we observe their appetite for the roots of our vegetables as they dig. Rarely will gophers risk rising above the ground to secure a delicious morsel of vegetation that their underground tunneling cannot reach. Rather, they will simply pull the vegetation into their tunnel from below. Artichokes are the gopher's favorite. Horrified, we witness our artichoke plants drooping in the sun after having been robbed of roots, their underground support and nutritional supply, by our long-toothed, burrowing guests. Neither we nor our garden can tolerate this destruction. We know we need to take action.

With our action, however, we must dig deeper than our gopher companions. Seeing the challenge before us as an opportunity to practice our mindfulness, we take a breath before addressing the tenacious appetite of our gophers. Our movements are decisive, skillful, and compassionate, with the clear intention of finding a harmonious solution for all involved—artichoke, gopher, and ourselves. Committed to seeing all life as our teacher, and dedicated to being a bodhisattva in our garden, extermination is not an option.

Continuing to breathe, we discover our gopher locals cannot chew their way past wire mesh. Using the wire mesh, we begin to set boundaries with them. Planting our trees and shrubs in wire baskets with mesh small enough, one-fourth to one-half inch, will keep our garden from being the gopher's lunch time buffet. Wire mesh can also be placed horizontally across the ground approximately six to eight inches below the surface to secure our larger mass plantings of vegetables and flowers. Decorative containers can serve as an aesthetically pleasing solution for keeping our gopher friends away from our plant's root systems as well. Setting boundaries allows us to live harmoniously with our native gophers as we recognize the land belongs to all beings, plants, and minerals. Moving as compassionate warriors, staying open and flexible, we learn how to resolve conflicts with even our most plundering guests, and we find ways to live together.

Some pillaging may even benefit our garden, like that of the green lacewings. The lacewings are nicknamed *Aphid lions* because they have a voracious appetite for aphids such as the armyworm. The army-worm will destroy an entire crop, eating everything before moving as an "army" to another area. Lace-wings are a natural predator to the armyworm, and while they are an insect, they are also our garden's ally. Understanding the balance of nature, we learn to pace ourselves, and to align our movements with the primal character of the natural world. As we learn to live in harmony with all the animals, insects, and fungi of our garden, we honor all life everywhere.

Knowing we are all guests,
Breathing in, we honor and acknowledge the ancient presence of our garden's inhabitants. We are all guests in our garden.

I look with the eyes of my heart.
Recognizing that all of life is innately and intimately interconnected, we release our desire for control and revenge. Breathing out, all of our thoughts, words, and actions are filled with compassion.

A compassionate warrior,
Breathing in, we turn toward our guests with the understanding of our bodhisattva nature.

I honor all life.
As a compassionate warrior our thoughts, motivations, and movements are embodied with deep understanding. Breathing out, we honor all life.

chapter 9

BLOOM!

Thank you, dear flower,
for making life so beautiful.
In your pure presence
I see my true self.

PURE PRESENCE

We can tend to the weeds and the watering of our garden with mindfulness, but the already present flower within the plant, and within ourselves, blooms in its own time. The first flowers in our garden often touch us immediately with their beauty. If we get closer, inhaling deeply, their fragrance can become part of us, and we can gently touch their velvety petals. The flower's beauty is a mirror of our own true beautiful nature. Beyond their physical appearance, beyond any story we tell ourselves about flowers and their character, they model pure presence, the beauty of simply being what they are, without vanity or apology.

Such is their presence, that if we take the time to truly see a flower, we can witness all of life in a single petal. Living there in the whorl of its fold lives the earth, the sky, and the sea. So too, lives the sun, the rain, and the heart of our labors tending its growth. We are in the flower, and the flower is in us. They arrive when sugar produced by photosynthesis within the leaves of the plant meets with mineral salts being drawn up from the soil by the plant's root system. Knowing a flower in this intimate detail—its wisdom to know when to grow and when to bloom—opens us. It changes us.

Flowers silently have the ability to transform our mood and inspire us with their beauty. The sun and the moon, the wind and the rain, are all held in the open heart of a flower. When we truly see a flower, we know we are looking into the face of true presence.

Thank you, dear flower,
Breathing in, we give thanks to the flowers in our garden. We know we have much to learn from their presence. Returning to our breath reminds us to appreciate their radiant beauty alive in their simple being.

for making life so beautiful.
Breathing out, we are thankful for the grace flowers add to our life. With our breath we share our thankfulness with our roses, orange blossoms, and our passion vines. They add so much joy to our lives.

In your pure presence
Breathing in, we notice the stillness of the flowers. Lying there in the belly of their petals lives pure presence. We breathe this presence into our very cells.

I see my true self.
Breathing out, we experience a deep resonance with the flower's simple being. The harmony we feel in witnessing a flower's essential nature is a clear mirror of our own true self.

BE THE BLOOM

Dear garden,
you mirror my heart.
With each beat,
a flower blooms.

In our garden, each stone turned reflects an obstacle we have overcome. Each weed removed mirrors our own mental clearing, and each flower's blooming is a blossoming of the qualities of understanding and compassion within ourselves. The garden is as much a mirror of our hearts as it is a manifestation of our vision. With each beat of our hearts a flower blooms, and as the gardener grows the garden, the garden grows the gardener.

Immersed in the life of our sanctuary, its wild vines tenderly wrapping their stories around our hearts, and the aspen's leaves quaking in the summer wind, like a grateful audience applauding our perspiration and labors on its behalf, our garden is a bridge between our inner and outer worlds. Giving our life force to the cultivation of our garden with focused attention and awareness, we evolve too. From its very roots, gardening serves the blossoming of our true nature—our basic goodness. Mindfully digging, planting, weeding, and pruning in our garden, our thoughts, words, and actions become more sensitive and authentic, and we grow in understanding, insight, and compassion. We

learn to respond to what is rather than impose ourselves—our preconceived ideas and perceptions—on
the environment, both inner and outer. Our sanctuary's
flowers paint the beauty of our hearts upon the wind
and the sky for all to witness. Life force to life force we,
and our garden, bloom.

Dear garden,
Breathing in, we devote our earthly labors—our backs,
hands, perspiration, and our hearts—to our garden.
Through our mindful gardening, we enter a sacred relationship with the land and its inhabitants, and our garden
becomes a place of deep connection and belonging.

you mirror my heart.
Breathing out, in the still presence and beauty of
each red, purple, and royal blue flower in the garden,
our mindfulness is reflected to us. The purity of each
flower's whorl, cups our basic goodness like dew to the
morning's sun, free for the offering. Breathing out, we
give ourselves over and over to our garden, to the sky,
and to all beings.

With each beat,
Breathing in, we offer kindness, generosity, and compassion for the Earth and all its inhabitants. Our gardens
allow us the opportunity to offer our essential goodness
to the natural world through our feet, our hands, and
our hearts.

a flower blooms.
Breathing out, our love lingers in the flower's fragrance—a testimony to our presence and theirs.

THE BEAUTY OF IMPERMANENCE

Beautiful flower,
you teach me so much.
May your equanimity ground me
in the face of life's impermanence.

As we watch the beauty of a flower come to life in our garden, we are often touched by the brevity of its visit. Soon the flower's petals will float to the hungry earth, becoming compost for next year's garden. From the opening of the bud to the dropping of the petals, we witness the unfurling grace of impermanence.

Like the flower, our bodies are of the nature to grow old, die, and be cast off. There is no way for us to escape our body growing old, deteriorating, and dying. Death is a part of life. The flower does not mind its impermanent nature and is never moved to complain. There is great wisdom in its equanimity. The flower's elegant entry and departure in our garden offer us an example of how to gracefully embrace the impermanence of life, including our own.

The rudimentary function of a flower is to provide

seed for its continuation into the next generation. However, through experiencing the memory of a beautiful gardenia—its soft cream-white color, its sweet fragrance, the perfection of its petals—we know the gardenia continues on in us as well. All that is dear to us, and everything and everyone we love, are of the nature to change and to be physically separated from us. Just as the gardenia lives on in us long after it has withered and fallen to the ground, our loved ones also live on in us. Memories—words, scents, hugs, and emotions—live on in our heart and body long after we have parted. In this graceful way flowers teach us the art of living beautifully with impermanence.

Beautiful flower,
Breathing in, we honor the beauty of our garden's flowers. Living such a short time, they offer a tender and beautiful reflection of life's impermanence. They are our teachers.

you teach me so much.
The flower's feathery form elegantly coming and going in our garden, we learn how to live surrendered to the truth of our own temporal physical existence. Breathing out, we stop fighting the flow of change.

May your equanimity ground me
Breathing in, we hold change with grace in the likeness of a flower.

in the face of life's impermanence.
Breathing out, we know the flower's equanimity is the seed of her continuation inside of us.

BENEATH THE BLOOM

> *Beneath every apple blossom*
> *lies the hidden seed of its continuation.*
> *Understanding the apple's wholeness*
> *is the fruit of our gardening.*

Beneath every apple blossom lies the hidden seed of its fruit. Given the right care, this seed will mature into a crisp, juicy fruit. The apple not only embodies the apple tree's flowers and houses the seeds for its own continuation, it provides sustenance for our bodies in the form of carbohydrates and fiber that give us energy. Upon its consumption, our thoughts, words, and actions are energized by the nutrition of the apple. The apple is part of us.

All of life is interconnected in this way. Thich Nhat Hanh says, "The bread you hold in your hands is the body of the cosmos." The sun, the sky, the clouds, the earth, the minerals, the farmer's hands, the field worker's labor in harvesting, the baker's skillfulness, the delivery person's safe driving, and the grocery store's stockers and cashiers come together to bring this bread into our hands. So many lives are inside one slice of bread, one apple, or a single flower.

Beneath every apple blossom

Lying beneath the beauty of a flower is the hidden potential and life of its seed. Only in dying to its present form can the flower allow the seed to thrive. Breathing in, we honor the wisdom of the flower to surrender.

lies the hidden seed of its continuation.

Carried in the flower is the seed, and carried in the seed is the continuation of the flower. Breathing out, we acknowledge the great cycle of life.

Understanding the apple's wholeness

Seeing how the flesh of an apple feeds us, energizes our minds, and fuels our actions, we gain insight into the interbeing of all life. Breathing in, we understand that we and the apple are part of the same whole.

is the fruit of our gardening.

Breathing out, we know, through our understanding and insight, we are a part of all of life. And like the apple, we mature into our own wholeness. This awakening is the real fruit of our gardening.

chapter 10

FINALLY
FRUIT

Honoring nature's wisdom,
I give my garden the space
to grow and mature.
Together, we bloom and bear fruit.

Receiving the fruits of our labor takes time. Our patience and contentment will allow our garden to prosper, grow, and produce its bounty. If we are impatient and tug upon the tender new shoots of our young plants, we will uproot the very growth we are intending to foster. Taking a step back, breathing, we give things time to mature, and we, too, grow and mature. As we tend to our garden's needs, weeding, watering, and composting, we keep a loving, dispassionate eye on our new residents. Like a parent who watches her child playing on the jungle gym from a distance, we give our plants the space and time they require to grow and express themselves, ready to step in if they are in danger.

Danger to a youthful garden may come in the form of inconsistent water, poor soil culture, crowding, insufficient light, or some combination of these obstacles. Remaining aware of the environmental conditions surrounding our newest additions, we allow them the greatest chance of fully maturing. Their fruits are theirs to offer, and will not arrive by force. We can only prepare the supportive conditions for their arrival. The rest we trust to the wisdom of nature.

Some plants have a very fast growing pattern, while others take their grand old time to mature. Herbs, like basil and mint, are fast growing. Their speedy growth allows us to enjoy their culinary delights and medicinal benefits within one growing season. A stone fruit or tree fruit, on the other hand, can take up to five to seven years to produce its fleshy, juicy rewards. If our eyes are focused only on the harvest, we will certainly become disenchanted with the slowness of our saplings. However, with our eyes turned inward, we can observe our own growth in the plants' reflection—their patterns, pauses, and natural tempo.

Sometimes we are like the herbs of our garden, and we learn and integrate life's lessons quickly and harvest their rewards. For example, imagine biting into a lemon for the first time: the shock of rushing right in, mouth wide for a big bite, anticipating it to be sweet like an orange, and being met by the sharp tartness of its tangy flesh. Immediately upon the lemon's arrival in our mouth, our taste buds announce its stinging sharpness to our tongue. We remember the shock. In the light of our experience, our next interlude with a lemon may be slower and more reserved, hesitating to rush into its pungent flavor. This is a lesson we learn quickly.

Other lessons take us more time to understand and integrate, like how to cultivate compassion when someone has caused us harm. It may take a few days, even several weeks, to fully understand the nature of our experience. Our insight develops in us slowly, more like the growth of stone fruit as opposed to an herb. However, with our mindful awareness we begin to understand the hurt and suffering within the one whom we perceive to have caused us harm, and we find compassion for him or her.

Change and growth follow their own timeline—in the garden and in the gardener. It is ours to give both our garden and ourselves space and time to unfold and mature naturally. In the open field of our mindfulness, together, we and our garden will bloom and bear fruit.

Honoring nature's wisdom,
Planting the seeds of our garden, we entrust ourselves to the earth's fold, its wisdom, and its ancient being. Breathing in, we know we have committed ourselves wisely.

I give my garden the space
Breathing out, we offer patience and contentment from our mindfulness practice, as we learn to release the outcome of our efforts into the Earth's all-knowing fold.

to grow and mature.
Breathing in, neither pulling nor pushing for a certain outcome, we are at ease and allow our garden and ourselves to unfold beautifully and naturally.

Together, we bloom and bear fruit.
Green, bloom, fruit is the rhythm of nature. Breathing out, we enjoy our fresh breath, completely alive in the present moment melody of our garden—green, bloom, fruit.

RIPENING WITH GRACE

Life comes together
in the flesh of my garden's fruit,
teaching me how
to ripen with grace.

Fruit is the coming together of sun, water, earth, minerals, and compost. Through its cherry tomatoes, aubergine eggplants, butter lettuce, chard, herbs, and red pears, our garden gracefully embodies the greatness of ripening. The rich flavors of our garden's vegetables and fruits are an eager testimony to the beauty and power of ripening with age, and the coming together of life.

Out of maturity, greatness—the flavor and juice of life—comes. Our garden's apples, oranges, and cherries teach us not to resist the unfoldment of our aging, but to ripen with grace into the truth of who and what we are. Like them, we patiently let the sun, the rain, the sky, and the earth of our garden mold us. It takes time to reveal our full shape and flavor—our greatness.

One apple seed may get planted where the soil is moist and soft, while another may be sown into soil that is rocky and dry. Each seed learns to thrive where it finds itself, and each becomes unique unto itself through its blessings and its challenges. Similarly, as we ripen, each cell of our body carries the unique experiences, understanding, and insights of our journey. We truly ripen when we humbly embrace the truth and wholeness of who and what we really are, offering it unabashedly to life around us. Learning not to resist our maturation— our true greatness—we ripen with grace.

To embrace our maturity—our wholeness—is to understand that we are a part of the continuum of the cosmos. Compost to soil, seed to sprout, bud to flower, flower to fruit, and fruit to compost, this is the unending circle of life and death. It is eternal, and so are we. Just as the fruits of our garden effortlessly offer their life force as nourishment and energy for our bodies, it is our task to discern our own unique purpose and expression as we mature. Sharing our wholeness, we mature with grace.

Life comes together
The earth, sun, moon, sky, wind, and rain all conspire to the coming together of life. Breathing in, we, too, conspire with nature in its grand expression.

in the flesh of my garden's fruit,
Breathing out, we are deeply aware of the totality of life living within a simple apple we hold in our hand.

teaching me how
Breathing in, we allow ourselves to ripen into our true self.

to ripen with grace.
Breathing out, surrendered to our natural unfolding and wholeness, we mature with grace.

FREE FALLING

Witnessing your humble surrender,
my sweet purple plum,
I free fall into being
that which I am, wherever I land.

Surrendering to the wisdom of the timeless wind, the plum falls to the earth without a whisper of complaint. On the ground, it will quickly become food for small animals, birds, and earthworms. If gathered in a basket, it may join its brothers and sisters in the making of a delicious pie. Harvested by our hand, warm with the sun, it may quench our thirst with its sweet juicy goodness on a bright summer day. The plum moves seamlessly from one form to another. Its *svadharma*—a Sanskrit word meaning "unique endeavor" or "life purpose"—is to simply be that which it is, wherever it finds itself. Each fruit and vegetable in our garden has its own svadharma to fulfill. Like the fruit of our garden, we too have our own unique purpose to express—a life force and gift that only we can offer. The uninhibited expression of our garden encourages us to surrender to and to fulfill our purpose wherever we find ourselves.

Witnessing your humble surrender,
Practicing mindfulness in the garden, we slow down to truly see the wonders of life surrounding us. Our slower

pace creates opportunities to witness the moment a plum releases its hold on the tree. Breathing in, we honor the plum's sweet surrender and humility as it touches the earth before us.

my sweet purple plum,
The plum is a dear friend of ours. Its humble life teaches us to softly surrender to who we really are. Breathing out, we offer our breath to the plum as a confirmation of our mindful attention and awareness of its silent message.

I free fall into being
In the plum's likeness, we can learn to allow ourselves the joy of free falling into our truest expression, our basic plum goodness. Breathing in, we acknowledge the truth of who we are.

that which I am, wherever I land.
We simply are that which we are. No effort is needed. Wherever we are, whatever we are doing, we have the opportunity to truly be ourselves. Breathing out, we relax into our being.

THE REAL FRUIT

Beloved garden,
because of who you are,
I am
who I am.

We are as much the fruit of our gardening as is the pomegranate growing on the tree's rugged branch. And in the pomegranate's likeness there are many ruby red seeds of goodness that have been planted within us through our mindfulness. As we garden, ours are the eyes that behold the beauty of nature and really see. Ours are the ears that learn to hear the language of the land and really listen, and ours are the hearts ready to receive the love and fruit of our garden's sanctuary and appreciate the absolute present moment they offer. Because of who you are, beloved garden, through our mindful weeding, pruning, digging, planting, and harvesting within your sanctuary, we can come to be who we are.

Beloved garden,
Our connection with the land has the potential to be as intimate and transforming as our relationships with other human beings. Breathing in, we acknowledge our relationship with our garden.

because of who you are,

Breathing out, we give thanks to our garden and the sanctuary it creates for us to simply be ourselves as we witness the surrender of a single plum falling to the earth, fulfilling its svadharma.

I am

Breathing in, we know that who and what we are is the real fruit of our gardening.

who I am.

Breathing out, we find peace in simply being who we are.

chapter 11

THE HEART OF THE HARVEST

*As my garden and I
unfold together,
authentic love
fills my heart.*

After all our work in our garden, it bears the physical gifts of our labors—gently tomentose string beans, smooth butternut squash, and the gnarled, dirty fingers of rainbow carrots—each with a story to tell like an old friend. We once held these plants as seeds, we nurtured them, and now they have been returned to us. Our gardening is relational and consequential—to the land, to ourselves, and to life. Like any good relationship, when we mindfully tend our garden, it nourishes us.

We, too, grow in the soil alongside the green bell peppers and red-skinned potatoes, the bright yellow daylilies and purple bearded iris. If we have watered and tended well, our arms fill over time with the jewels of golden muscat grapes, shiny maroon cherries, and sun-warmed plums to nourish our bodies, brilliant pink dahlias and lavender to fill our senses, and lemon balm and chamomile to calm our minds. Through its harvest, our garden teaches us the nature of true generosity. A relationship of dispassionate yet consequential reciprocity, generosity is born in the soil of our being, as we grow and unfold with our garden through our mindfulness practice. In the richness of this mutual exchange, authentic love grows, and in nature's likeness—knowing no withholding—we share our love with great generosity.

As my garden and I

Mindful gardening is the unfolding and interweaving of our life force with that of the Earth. Breathing in, we enter fully into an authentic relationship with our garden.

unfold together,

Our relationship with our garden is at once dispassionate and consequentially reciprocal. Breathing in, together, we sprout, grow, bloom, and fruit.

authentic love

What we do unto our land, we do unto ourselves. Breathing out, we vow to live beautifully in love with our garden.

fills my heart.

As we embrace our connection with all of life, it is our natural response to fall in love. This falling is the true heart of the harvest. Breathing out, we offer our love freely.

SURRENDERING SEPARATENESS

Holding a leaf in my hand,
I surrender my sense of separateness.
The cloud, the leaf, and I are connected.
We are, because everything else is.

Looking deeply at a leaf, we can see there is a cloud floating in its luminescent green face. Without the cloud, there would be no rain; and without rain, there would be no tree to grow such a beautiful leaf. If the cloud is not there, the leaf cannot be there. In turn, the water that evaporates from the leaf's surface creates moisture in the air, which returns to the sea and the clouds. The cloud and the leaf coexist and cocreate each other.

Looking at our hands, we can also see that the cloud and the leaf are there too. Holding a leaf, we see it is in our hands—literally and figuratively. With lobes like our fingers and veins like the patterns on our palms, the leaf gives us oxygen to nourish our cells and allows our bodies to thrive. It is very important to us. Without water, without the cloud, both we and the leaf could not live. The cloud is very important to us, too. Looking deeply, we can see that both the cloud and the leaf are in our hands.

Continuing to look, we can see our ancestors are also in our hands. We see them in the length and shape of our fingers and our palms. Without the cloud, without the leaf, without our ancestors, our hands could not exist. All of nature exists within our hands. In fact, we cannot look at a single leaf, flower, fruit, or insect in our garden without seeing everything—sun, warmth, sky, clouds, rain, earth, minerals, time, space—inside of it. Learning to see like this, we begin to merge our awareness with nature, and we learn to surrender our sense of separateness.

Holding a leaf in my hand
Breathing in, I see the cloud and the leaf are present in my hand, and my hand is in the leaf and in the cloud, too.

I surrender my sense of separateness.
Because we understand that when we perspire it evaporates to become a cloud, we know we are a part of the cloud. Because we planted the acorn that grew into the leafy tree, we can see we are also in the leaf. Breathing out, I see that I am in both the leaf and the cloud.

The cloud, the leaf, and I are connected.
Breathing in, I know I am not separate from nature.

We are because everything else is.
Breathing out, we acknowledge our presence in our connection to all of life.

LIVING LIFE LARGE

Understanding my connection with all of life,
I become an authentic gardener.
Free of fear
I live life large.

When we see with the eyes of understanding, we
become authentic gardeners. Looking at a flower, we
can see the compost. Looking at the compost, we can
see the flower. Immersed in our garden, we can see
all of life includes everything else timelessly. Steeped
in the wisdom of life's continuity, we practice mindful
reverence toward all beings, animals, plants, and minerals, making us wise and good gardeners. We carry the
knowledge that nothing lives separately, and nothing is
ever born or ever dies. Life is a continuation.

We are the earth, and we are the gardener. We are
the lotus and the mud, the hawk and the condor, the
butterfly and the stinkbug. Knowing that everything is
us, and we are everything, we see and experience life
as a generous continuation of giving and receiving.
Understanding who and what we are—one with life
itself—our gardening is selfless and neither expects nor
needs anything in return. We, in the likeness of our garden, learn to be immensely generous. We learn to give
freely of our love, our compassion, and our wisdom.
With the hands of our mindfulness, we sow the seeds

of our thoughts, words, and actions. They become our continuation, and our gift to all of life. We have become authentic gardeners, and through our mindfulness in the garden, we continue on beautifully into the future.

Understanding my connection with all of life,
Seeing the flower in the compost and the compost in the flower, we understand the interconnectedness of all of life. We are woven into and of nature's elements—earth, fire, water, and air. Breathing in, we understand we are an integral part of the whole.

I become an authentic gardener.
Breathing out, we let our insight and understanding guide our thoughts, words, and actions. We become more compassionate, kind, and patient, both in our gardens and in our lives. As these qualities are nurtured in us, we become authentic gardeners.

Free of fear
Breathing in, we commit ourselves to living mindfully, that we may understand our interconnectedness with all of life.

I live life large.
Breathing out, we vow to live large by giving our presence, our hearts, and our love generously to all of life. Love is our continuation through all beings, animals, plants, and minerals everywhere.

REFERENCES

Brenzel, Kathleen Norris. 2001. *Sunset Western Garden Book*. Menlo Park, CA: Sunset Publishing Corporation.

Johnson, Wendy. 2008. *Gardening at the Dragon's Gate: At Work in the Wild and Cultivated World*. New York: Bantam Dell.

Mabey, Richard. 2010. *Weeds: In Defense of Nature's Most Unloved Plants*. New York: Harper Collins Publishers.

Macy, Joanna. 1991. *World as Lover, World as Self*. Berkeley, CA: Parallax Press.

Mitchell, Stephen. 1999. *Tao Te Ching- Lao Tzu: An Illustrated Journey*. London, England: Frances Lincoln Limited.

Nhat Hanh, Thich. 1998. *Interbeing: Fourteen Guidelines for Engaged Buddhism*. Berkeley, CA: Parallax Press.

———. 2006. *The Energy of Prayer: How to Deepen Your Spiritual Practice*. Berkeley, CA: Parallax Press.

———. 2006. *Transformation and Healing*. Berkeley, CA: Parallax Press.

———. 2007. *Chanting from the Heart: Buddhist Ceremonies and Daily Practices*. Berkeley, CA: Parallax Press.

O'Brian, Ellen Grace. 1998. *Living the Eternal Way: Spiritual Meaning and Practice for Everyday Life*. San Jose, CA: Center for Spiritual Enlightenment Press.

———. 2002. *A Single Blade of Grass: Finding the Sacred in Everyday Life*. San Jose, CA: CSE Press.

Palmer, Parker J. 2004. *A Hidden Wholeness: The Journey toward an Undivided Life*. San Francisco, CA: John Wiley & Sons, Inc.

A Running Press Miniatures Edition. 1994. *Native American Wisdom*. Philadelphia, PA: Running Press Book Publishers.

Streep, Peg. 1999. *Spiritual Gardening: Creating Sacred Space Outdoors*. Makawao, Maui: Inner Ocean Publishing, Inc.

Photo © Natascha Bruckner

ZACHIAH LAURANN MURRAY is a Registered Landscape Architect and Certified Massage Therapist. A Masters of Divinity candidate in Meru Seminary, at The Center for Spiritual Enlightenment, she regularly teaches meditation classes for the community and outreach programs. She is a member of the Order of Interbeing in the lineage of Thich Nhat Hanh, and holds a second degree brown belt in Aikido, a nonviolent martial art seeking the harmonious resolution of conflict. She assists and teaches in the children's classes at Aikido of Santa Cruz where she trains regularly. She finds her home in a lovely cottage located in Santa Cruz, California, where the wild peacocks roam freely and often sleep in the redwoods above her roof.

JASON DeANTONIS is an award-winning sculptor and visual artist. His illustrations have appeared in galleries, art books, textbooks, novels, and children's books. His recent projects for Parallax Press include *Making Space: Creating a Home Meditation Practice* by Thich Nhat Hanh and *Little Pilgrim* by Ko Un. You can see more of his work at www.jasondeantonis.com.

NOTES

Parallax Press, a nonprofit organization, publishes books on engaged Buddhism and the practice of mindfulness by Thich Nhat Hanh and other authors. All of Thich Nhat Hanh's work is available at our online store and in our free catalog. For a copy of the catalog, please contact:

Parallax Press
www.parallax.org
P.O. Box 7355
Berkeley, CA 94707
Tel: (510) 525-0101

Monastics and laypeople practice the art of mindful living in the tradition of Thich Nhat Hanh at retreat communities worldwide. To reach any of these communities, or for information about individuals and families joining for a practice period, please contact:

Plum Village
13 Martineau
33580 Dieulivol, France
www.plumvillage.org

Blue Cliff Monastery
3 Mindfulness Road
Pine Bush, NY 12566
www.bluecliffmonastery.org

Magnolia Grove Monastery
123 Towles Rd.
Batesville, MS 38606
www.magnoliagrovemonastery.org

Deer Park Monastery
2499 Melru Lane
Escondido, CA 92026
www.deerparkmonastery.org

The Mindfulness Bell, a journal of the art of mindful living in the tradition of Thich Nhat Hanh, is published three times a year by Plum Village. To subscribe or to see the worldwide directory of Sanghas, visit www.mindfulnessbell.org

635
MUR

Murray, Zachiah.

Mindfulness in the
  garden.

$16.95